They Didn't Tell Us

They Didn't Tell Us

Shan Tolbert

1

Heal

2

Love & Affection

3

I Ain't Mad at you

4

It's Personal

5

Pain Can Change

6

Seasons

7

Not The Same

8

What's Next?

Forward

I met Shantanique when she was in the second or first grade. Her older cousin Britney went to Cooper so she followed not long after. Just like most kids, I encounter Shantanique became one of my children. She later told me she wanted to try out for basketball. She came in the 3rd grade and tried out. I cut her that year. She then came back the next year and made the team. But the year she made the team she rode the bench most of that year. But that 5th-grade year, Shantanique came back a player. She had learned the game. She had developed a little more over the summer and she was tough. It was her time. I tell this story one because I am the only coach that can say I ever cut her. She always says that after that moment she never wanted to feel that again so every summer she focused on getting better. Shan has played with the best of the best and even though undersized she continued to excel in that area of her life. It's not about talent. Shan has a determination about her that doesn't allow her to accept defeat. She doesn't give excuses she just does what needs to be done and waits until her moment. And in most cases when it's her moment not only will she know it.. but you will too.

Ms. Tolbert is a young lady that I have had a front-row seat at seeing the growth since the age of 6 years old. She has always had this nothing is going to stop me aura about herself. From falling on the basketball court numerous times to falling in life, she has gotten up every time with a determination that is prepared for more. She literally gets stronger with every fall. No injury nor physical issue (Asthma) would be an excuse for why she could not accomplish whatever she set her mind to. Driven people like Shantanique get up every day with a prepared plan and won't sleep until each task is completed. I love you kid and me saying I'm proud of you just won't give enough justice. Thank you for letting me be a part of your journey so far.

This is your time. Your moment

Shaw.

Heal

They didn't tell us

Untreated trauma will always reveal itself.

Deal with you before the world has to

Nobody is responsible for your healing but you!

Pain can be turned into positive energy.

I was molested!!! Whew, It's out now lol. The cat is out of the bag. Now I wanted to start this off this way because I know this news may rock my family to the core. I am not going to apologize for waiting to reveal this until now because I need my family, as well as all other black families, to understand the effect this kind of trauma can have on a child's mind. This chapter is probably the hardest thing I've ever had to do. But it's necessary, it's necessary not only for me currently but the future me as well. I've learned that you if don't deal with things from your past, they show up in your future and no matter how late they come, they come. To be completely honest this is something that I always thought I would take to my grave. I didn't think I would ever tell a soul that I went through this. The reason being is because my family or I guess most black families, think stuff like this is not supposed to happen or doesn't happen.

The crazy thing is it happens a lot more often in African-American families overall just don't talk about it. When a child comes forth sometimes stuff gets swept under the rug and then a child is in a battle with their family as well as themselves. This is how kids go through life and get hooked on drugs and alcohol because they are trying to cope with childhood trauma that they were forced to keep to themselves. The fear of not wanting the family to look bad or for people to be in your business has kept a lot of BS hidden. The problem is you save the face of the family but you break the soul of that child. This usually takes them down a long road of hiding pain to save face later in life as well. But the thing with Trauma is it always shows itself. It's never really fully hidden. When it comes to sexual childhood trauma that could lead to so many things including addictions, toxic behavior in relationships/friendships, or it could affect your sexual life. Most people who deal with childhood sexual trauma go one or two ways. They are either extremely hyper-sexual or extremely reserved.

For about seven years of my life, I was molested continuously and when it finally stopped it was around the time that I was getting my first boyfriend. I had begun to reach the stage of maturity where I could say no and feel comfortable and get myself out of the situation a little bit more often. At this point, I knew it's wrong like in my head I could identify with the fact that this has to stop. As a child I can tell you because it started with me at such an early age, you have so many mixed emotions about what is happening. It's hard to decipher what is literally right from wrong. This is the case especially when the person who hurts you is extremely close to you. My first perception of it was "This is going to break my family apart if I say anything". Even up until recently when I was able to tell my Mother I still carried that fear. My family means the world to me so I couldn't imagine myself being the reason everybody was upset about something. Ain't that interesting even still? That I would believe my truth wasn't important enough to reveal out of the protection of someone else? Family or not that's a bad place to start your childhood because it will carry on into your adulthood. You know this shouldn't be happening because of who this person is but your brain is not mature enough to process how wrong this situation is If that makes sense. I thought that I wouldn't have to deal with it anymore but seeds were planted that I wouldn't see grow until I got older.

Oh, you a Tomboy!

Growing up I wasn't much of a girly girl and a lot of people didn't know that my being molested played a big role in it. See when you go through a Traumatic situation that takes away your innocence and you haven't developed and matured and become confident in who you are it affects you. So that self-confidence and acknowledgment of self are places where you're going to struggle. I know most people believed my story that I picked up a ball because I was with my cousins and friends in the neighborhood but truthfully I was trying to find something that

Shan Tolbert

would make me stand out but protect me at the same time. See in my young mind because of what I was going through… I didn't feel pretty, I honestly didn't like ANYTHING about myself except my hair. I figured if I bond with the boys they won't like me in a way that they would hurt me like I was being hurt at home and that instead, they would protect me as one of "the homies". So in a sense me being a Tomboy was a defense mechanism.

Growing up I felt like my cousin was the pretty one and I was just there. She was chocolate and had long hair she use to wear in a wrap. She was little and she was petite. Everybody just thought she was so beautiful, shit I thought she was beautiful. But the looks the males gave her or the attention she got from people, in general, I didn't get. This is one of the ways that trauma usually affects young girls or young people. We start kind of developing an identity crisis. I picked up the ball to try to develop something that would help me stand out to people. Then I eventually started to get good at it. People started to notice when I started playing well. Then I started to get noticed because I'm hanging around the guys a lot more because of basketball so they are getting to know me and when they get to know me they started liking me. So the Tom Boy thing kind of started working in my favor with getting the attention of the guys. But the problem with that attention is these guys were not looking to be my boyfriend. It's crazy to say that these guys were looking for somebody to give them some or to get some head. These weird young elementary/middle school relationships where behind closed doors they tell you they like you and that you're pretty and blah blah but when you get out around your friends or in public they don't even acknowledge you or when somebody asks are y'all together they say no. I can't tell you how many times I went through that type of humiliation at a young age. It's so funny to be talking about this because I've experienced this same type of rejection probably more as an adult than I did as a kid. So that sting is still very relevant to me. I was cool, I was ok looking but not ok enough for them to like me like that. It's a complex feeling somewhere between, "I want you to like me so that I know that nothing is wrong with me. Because the person who "liking me" this way at home ain't suppose to be, so "like me for real so I can know other people do". Then it gives the feeling of, "I want you to like me but don't hurt me like what I'm going through... I might kiss you but I don't wanna do anything else because That hurts me.. but oh if I don't do anything else you not gonna like me? So let me do just enough to see where this goes". Man, that's an exhausting cycle to be in. But that's where I was and mentally where I've been up until I was 26 years old. A lot of people didn't know that I was extremely boy crazy at a very young age and I got myself in a lot of sticky situations trying to see if somebody saw more than I saw in myself. I started this search for love very early and I was getting my feelings crushed. More and more my self-esteem was being shattered and I couldn't see myself more than the Tomboy who played basketball. I was good. I was a star athlete, a smart chick they could use to cheat off my paper and all that but I wasn't the pretty girl that they wanted to claim. Aside from the tomboy thing in connection with basketball I also did not like the attention that came with when I dressed a certain way. It's crazy to me to say this now but this is just really how I felt but I wanted dudes to still like me. Believe me, as confused as you are reading this this is exactly how confused I felt. All I can say is this was the mind of a child who was emotionally traumatized but mentally present. I knew what I liked or didn't like, but I wanted to be liked as well, but not for what other girls were liked for. I wanted to be liked. But I couldn't figure out how to hold on to that innocence without compromising my body. I wasn't having sex yet but I was engaging in things I had no business doing trying to keep people. So when it came to dressing a certain way that attention was overwhelming to me because it's never the type of attention I wanted. I didn't want to be over-sexualized. I didn't want them to look at my body or if I had a little dress or if my boobs were showing, those things made me feel so outside of myself and exposed. I struggled with it all the way through high school and even still do now. I'm very conscious of what I wear. So I figured if I dress like a tomboy the maybe someone would get to know me and just like me and I wouldn't have to do all that extra stuff. But that honestly didn't happen so I began to compromise more and more as I got older.

It's your fault (Daddy issues)

During the time of me being boy crazy, I was also in a season of my life where my dad wasn't really around. When you go through a traumatic experience such as the one that I just talked about, your anger has to go somewhere. And because this was the man that I'm told is appointed to me, this is my father, this is the person that's supposed to protect me and he wasn't there....That's where my anger went. So on top of Him not being around I was angry at him for not being there to protect me. But the tricky thing with trauma and anger is you go looking for the love that you didn't get or that protection you didn't get in other males. The moment a male makes you feel comfortable or protected, you fall from them. Not truly knowing that person's intentions. I can say I grew attached at an extremely young age because of this. I was getting strong with cutting the trauma at home but all I was doing was reverting the toxic trait I had picked up from it elsewhere. I'm talking about whatever you want me to do except have sex with you, Ima do it because I don't want you to leave. Because you tell me you care about me and you tell me you really like me and I want you to like me so I do it. Then I got to the end of these situations and I still ended up alone.

While I am writing this, that same empty Pit feeling in my stomach that I used to get during this time I'm starting to feel it as I'm writing. The reality of what I was searching for was my dad, that love that showed me that I was beautiful, that love that assured me of who I was wasn't there. So it is funny to me now because I always tell people at this time I was a virgin but I wasn't innocent. I was far from it actually. I spent most of my adolescence Just trying to feel my way to love, or at least what I thought was love. I wanted to know that what happened to me didn't matter and that I was somebody that they wanted to show off to their friends and family. I wanted to know what happened to me and didn't take away the fact that I was an amazing person. If you get to know me you will really love me. But kids are shallow LOL. Kids are not thinking at all that she has a great personality so she's going to make a great girlfriend. I wasn't wearing tight jeans or skirts or anything like that so I didn't get in public what I got behind closed doors.

Alexa play Xscape- My little secret! lol.

Eventually, I just rolled with it because I just wanted to feel something and that was the beginning of me settling in hopes of just getting a small taste of a feeling. One of my favorite groups of all time is Jagged edge. They have a song called "What's it like to be in love", and till this day that one part that goes "I was just wondering, will love ever know me. Well my heart is open and I've been hoping...To find what it is everybody keeps on talking bout", gets me every time.

26 (May 24)

Whew, so let's recap here. I was molested as a child. I want boys to like me. But I'm dressing like them because I don't want sexual attention. I'm doing whatever a boy asks me to do because I want them in my life. I miss my daddy, but he wasn't there to protect me from being molested so I'm slick mad at him. All of these things have been the breeding ground for rejection issues, low self-esteem, abandonment issues, and misguided affection. Even through years of being in a cycle with all those things I didn't lose my virginity until I was 26 years old. I know most will read this like well that's a good thing, ehh maybe it is maybe it isn't. I still was being dumb without having sex so could you imagine the dumbness I was getting ready to get into once I got "outside" as we will call it lol. This wasn't so much an intentional walk as it was me

1. Never getting comfortable enough with a dude to allow it to happen,

2. I gave a lot of dudes blue balls because I knew how to stop the show when I began to get uncomfortable (Which was usually from the beginning). Or

3. Me being afraid of who I would become once I started.

I was very self-aware. I knew my flawed areas and they had been used against me in my past I just knew I wasn't ready for the hurt that would come with being "outside". I used to have a lot of people ask me did I save myself for marriage. At this point, my faith was beginning to blossom and grow but I can assure you that wasn't the case. Because of the trauma that I encountered, I had an extremely hard time getting comfortable. So when I was old enough and I was actually dating throughout high school and college I just kept dudes at a distance using my basketball career and school as my excuse. After many years since going through the molestation, I stopped thinking about it, I just wanted to move on with my life. I was growing into a young woman and was starting to have some fun so I just wanted to enjoy that feeling without the attachment of that stain. I thought I had completely deleted that situation out of my head but trauma just doesn't work like that. So I wasn't realizing it was manifesting in my young adulthood. I used to date but I wasn't having sex so that cost me a lot of relationships at least so I thought. This was one of the main reasons no one saw me in a serious relationship during my high school years or even college. I was completely focused on basketball so I'm not gonna necessarily say this was the case with college but definitely for high school. I would try hard every time I got into a situation to relax and you know just do it like Nike lol, and it just would not happen. So I just stopped putting myself in those situations and started figuring out how to convince dudes to do what I wanted without having to have sex. Again as good as that may sound, that's just my toxic behavior growing. This made me feel in control and after getting what I wanted I didn't create any attachments to these guys. I started being able to engage in certain activities without growing feelings or even wanting to see that person again. What a full 180 huh? I went from wanting the attention and doing things to get and keep it, to getting what I wanted and not wanting to become emotionally attached out of the fear of eventually being rejected and abandoned. So after making it through my dumb young years in high school and college I still wasn't having intercourse. I kind of got to the point where it was just like whatever.

After I graduated from undergrad I ended up moving back home for three years and in one of those years I ended up meeting the young man I would eventually lose my virginity to. It is hilarious to me that people always say when a young girl starts dating they usually date guys who have characteristics of their father and I can genuinely say this person definitely has a lot of mannerisms of my father. I tried to ignore it because I was so physically attracted to this dude. With all the problems I had internally, my female intuition and even this person himself, warned me that this was not the situation for me. But my low self-esteem and lack of self-value put me in a position to be the pursuer instead of being pursued. Now you may be thinking "Well what does that have to do with this situation". Women, Men are natural hunters. Young ladies never pursue, you are the prize, you are the gift, you are what a good man finds. I tried to trick myself into avoiding being put in a position to be hurt, so I called myself taking over the situation by going after what I wanted. If I made the first move enough and got turned down enough it would kill my expectations when a guy actually accepted my pursuit. I referred to this idea as the fishing theory. I always say God made a lot of fish in the sea, if you don't catch one, throw the reel out and keep fishing. Now, I'm not gonna lie. I still live by this theory lol but I approach it completely differently now. This method worked for a while, but I started noticing none of these situations were lasting. Either later the dude just lost interest or I did, or the situation just was not it and I would have been settling had I stayed in it. But with this particular person, this dude was so fine to me. Like legit One of the most handsome dudes in the world. I think it was more of a challenge to me to see if I could pull somebody this fine. From the day I saw him I told myself I just had to see. I just wanna introduce myself. I won't do anything more than that, and I did. I introduced myself and that was it. The problem was later on we began to be around each other a little bit more and we started to have conversations. I am a sucker for intellect and I'm a sucker for people who have the same passions as me. Coming into the work I was coming into, I learned that I had a passion for kids. This particular person did as well and a lot of my goals and things that I wanted to do as far as nonprofit and everything he had the same passion and goals so those were the things that connected us. The connection should've stopped there LOL. But truthfully I can honestly say this whole situation I pursued. I just kept flirting having regular conversations and then one day I remember asking for his number for something about mentoring or something. Initially, I did only contact him for that for a while, and then I shot my shot. But when I shot my shot he didn't turn me down he flirted back so that was my green light to keep flirting lol. Eventually, the flirting wouldn't just stay there. We started hanging out even more but it just didn't go past the flirting. I'm not gonna lie, I don't remember when the flirting turned into other things but he gave me a ride home one day and we were talking and we kissed. I think it just took root from that moment. That one kiss turned into kisses before we left each other's presence. That turned into us sneaking off just to have a kiss. I can remember I was so physically attracted to this man that when I would get in those close spaces with him my heart rate would shoot through the roof. It was so weird because I have never experienced any crap like that before. Like see somebody and just start sweating because your body temperature rising. Now here's another thing ladies/ Gentleman, let me tell you that is not love. Your body reacting to somebody in that manner is 100% Lust. That is common sense leaving your body expeditiously!! After that kiss, we begin to talk on the phone and have certain conversations and I remember him vividly telling me he wasn't ready for a relationship and I just was like OK. But being like most women who couldn't see past what I wanted I told him I would wait but all the while still trying to pressure him into one later on. I wanted to talk and now that I've gone through the process I kinda wish I would've listened to him. If a dude is constantly telling you that he's not ready for a relationship or he is saying things like he's scared of you or he's scared of the situation or if it makes him nervous those are legit red flags. You definitely should pay attention to these things. That is a dudes way of trying to honestly tell you that they may want a situation...just not with you. Not saying anything wrong with you but you could just not be what they want at that point in their lives. I can honestly say with this person I still believe he has an amazing heart. Eventually, he's going to make an amazing husband but he was honest and I was so caught up in what I wanted and how he made me feel and butterflies with a sprinkle of lies and now we have soul ties lol. So long story short this flirting and just turned into random kissing and that went on for about two years and eventually we just kind of started spending time with each other outside of our everyday situation. Things were progressing at least so I thought lol. I just knew the way we were moving that we was on our way to being in a relationship. He had met my mom, now given it was because he was leaving out of the house one day and she ended up coming home, but he still met her so this was serious.

Alexa Play... Rocko- Going Steady! lol

Eventually, we were in a situation where we ended up having sex. At this point, I just knew I was in love with him and I knew he had some messiness to him but I really really liked him. Even though different things that we had encountered at the time told me I should've gotten away, I got closer. I had done it, I lost my virginity. Not long after I found out that he was in a full-blown relationship that was kind of downplayed as he was just talking to other people which I wasn't tripping about because I was talking to other people, but I'm talking about a full-blown matching outfits type relationship. I was crushed! Well Kinda, I was more hurt that the seriousness of the situation wasn't disclosed. So that of course made me feel like a homewrecker. But just like the same cycle I put myself in as a child trying to get people to like me, this was no different. The thing with losing my virginity at such a later age I thought that I should've known better than the things that followed after losing my virginity. I felt like a lot of the mistakes I made at this time I should've made when I was 18,19 years old. But because of the way I was moving at that age I was falling into a full-blown stupid head mode when I should've been full grown. At least that's how I felt about the situation but, Not only did I continue to have sex with this person while knowing he was in a relationship but I put myself at risk to be hurt more emotionally and even putting my whole body at risk by continuing to play with this fire unprotected. My self-esteem was so shattered at this point I didn't care that he was in a relationship. I knew how I felt about him and if he was going to continue to come after me for sexual encounters I would continue to give them to him because it made me feel something. It made me feel wanted. He made me feel beautiful, I wasn't ready to give that up. No matter how messy I knew the situation was, I just wasn't willing to give up this feeling just yet. Eventually, he started to be a lot more flirtatious and I loved the attention. Getting stuff for Valentine's Day, little teddy bears, chocolate, little notes left for me. Now that I look back he was literally doing the bare minimum but he was doing it. We even engaged in conversations about potentially have a kid, nothing too serious but we entertained a few conversations. Looking back now I just kind of laugh because I was so caught up physically in that man I couldn't see past the foolishness that I had allowed myself to get entangled in. I know a lot of people who are going to read this and be like "Man, I didn't even know she was cut like that". To be honest I didn't know I was cut like that. But that's what not loving yourself and not knowing who you are or your value can get you. In a place where you don't recognize who you are. It can get you in a place where you forget who you belong to. Forgetting you are a daughter of the King and that you deserve happiness. You deserve to feel things but you deserve to feel those things from somebody who is only about you. This situation begin to get a little messier and I slowly just started to remove myself from it. A lot of lessons I was leaving it with but I was finally strong enough to separate myself from it. After this situation, I can genuinely say I did a lot of self-reflecting and a lot of crying and just trying to understand myself and how I could allow myself to get into something like that.

I wanted to be completely honest in this particular section of the book because I wouldn't dare put all of this blame on this young man as a lot of women do. A lot of us have to take responsibility for our toxic behavior and situations as well and this was my opportunity to do that and to show us as young women that sometimes the mess that we get ourselves into is not the result of another person, but the result of us. That boy did not force me to do anything that I didn't want to do, he wasn't the one that pursued me. I continued to pursue him and it was like eventually he just gave in. Although we did get to a point where I think we had mutual feelings for each other, my feelings were a lot stronger than his. Had my feelings not been so strong and full of lust I would've been able to avoid a lot of heartache in that situation. But I tell people all the time I don't regret the person that I lost my virginity to because again I still think he is an amazing dude and eventually he's going to grow into exactly what God wants him to be but that was just not for me. He wasn't for me no matter how much I tried to manipulate the situation into what I thought it should be. I just wasn't it. Maybe I wouldn't have gone through the pain that I had to go through. But I don't regret him. I regret the circumstances and as an adult, I have to take responsibility for the part that I play in all circumstances as well.

PTSD

So after completely removing myself from that situation, I found myself in another situation with a friend of mine. I and this particular person had grown extremely close in our years and became best friends to a certain extent. But he was in a relationship and at one point in our friendship I didn't even think our relationship would be any more than just that. We were just cool. Eventually, he started to show a little bit more feelings and things towards me and I would always like to down-play them because I knew he had a whole situation at home and I just got out of a messy situation so I wasn't looking to find another one. They would be on and off a lot and this is when he would show me the most affection and just always try to do extra things.

While they were together even if I called him at 3 a.m. and said I was stranded or if I needed anything he would leave their house and come bring it to me or come get me or whatever. We had never done anything and I planned on keeping it that way. So one particular night while they were broken up and he had moved out and everything. He asked me to come over and something started happening and I began to have flashbacks of being molested. I expressed my discomfort. I got up and stormed out of the house. On my way home I was hysterical. I was just crying and screaming, it literally felt like a movie. He called and called but I could not communicate what the problem was, I couldn't even put it into words. When I got home I called my best friend and I screamed and cried some more. I told her what the issue was and how I was uncomfortable and restricted and it took me right back to being a child and being in those situations. This was the first time I had experienced PTSD. I lost it and I couldn't express why I had lost it. So I blocked him off my phone that night and I left him blocked for about six months. I was so distraught and traumatized I didn't want to look at this man let alone answer a phone call. It wasn't even that he had done anything crazy it literally just came out of nowhere. So here's where the toxic part of being a woman comes in because after six months I took the man off the block list and called him one day like nothing had happened. After I felt like I was calm I was ready to talk, well he was pissed. He was pissed that I shut him out, he was pissed that I didn't tell him what was wrong. He said, "I can't understand how you can just block me out of your life like that". But I couldn't explain it, I was literally having a traumatic moment and couldn't create words to express it. We were able to finally have a conversation about it in a calm tone and I was able to express my issues and all those things and he was able to listen. I think we got a mutual understanding but our relationship literally never was the same after that. This particular manifestation of my trauma showed me that its levels to trauma.

Now that I was sexually active it was showing itself differently. I've never screamed and cried the way I did that night. I couldn't explain it because it had never happened to me before. So although I feel like I lost somebody that was extremely important to me I feel like I gained myself in that situation. I gained myself in the manner that I understood that trauma comes with triggers that you may not know are there until you get in certain situations. I was understanding that triggers come in all shapes and sizes and different forms at every level of my life. I could potentially run into a trigger that I didn't know existed because it was a phase in my life that I hadn't experienced. Once I begin to actually have sex and have meaningful relationships or situationships I started to see my emotions about certain things. It was hard for me to show emotions or wanna show the dude I was there because I had a history of people acting like they cared about me and leave me. So that triggered me to always be defensive and I would only let the situation get so far. I would try to control it as much as possible. I didn't know what to do in the situation when it would get out of my control. I would start separating myself so that I could walk away. I'd like to think those times in my life were a lot simpler. I was really good at dating but I just didn't know how or want to commit. I was terrified of somebody playing with me. That was one of my biggest fears so I started playing the game like a dude. As a means to protect me, I didn't know that I was just putting a Band-Aid over an infected area that needed to be dealt with and healed properly. If you notice while reading I went through these different phases of how I viewed relationships but none of them were healthy. One was always a coping mechanism as a result of the last one.

Lessons Learned

When you go through all of these different levels that I just described you start developing these deep scars that are kind of hard for you to explain. When you have a trauma of being molested or raped or anything like that I explain it to people this way: It feels like you have a stain on you that you spend your whole life trying to cover up because you don't want to seem damaged, but the problem is every time you try to cover it, it starts to move. The stain might be on your right shoulder if you cover it up but then it moves to the side of your face. It's like you don't want anybody to see the secret that you are carrying around but because you have so many undealt with emotions that stain grows. It grows into a bigger thing that you can no longer cover. They see it in these flaws and the problem with that is people could use these flaws as a benefit for them. That's how you get into the situations where dudes are using you just for sex or really are using you for pleasurable games or you find yourself doing whatever just to have a man/woman in your life. The stain makes you feel unworthy of love and makes you feel like you are going to be in a situation where you have to accept whoever is willing to accept you. It literally makes you feel like second-best and as I'm writing this I am coming to the realization that those feelings of feeling second best are not new. It's literally the exact emotion I went through with myself while growing up comparing myself to my cousin. The scary part with things like this is it can trickle over into your relationships and those people who are close to you, you watch them do all the dirt in the world and they end up in these great relationships that feeling comes up then. Things are working out in their lives as far as having kids, their love lives are thriving and you on the other hand have to work hard not to fall into jealously. What I need people to understand is the jealousy is not out of being jealous of your loved ones, the jealousy stems from hurt. When you hurt so young and then spend your whole life trying to be this good person and nothing good comes out of it for you it makes you think, "well I should have lived my life the way they did instead of tryna do it the right way". But if I learned anything about perception during this year alone it is that Doing right and having the Right intentions are two completely different things. I carried myself in a good manner, a great manner some would say. But my heart wasn't right. My heart was in comparison mode all the time. My heart was doing things for the people I loved to make me feel good about myself and when I wasn't doing things for them I felt empty. It's hard to be truly happy for your loved ones when you are internalizing their happiness the wrong way because of your hurt. Then getting in relationships feels like you are losing them. The dynamic of your relationships changing hurts more than you can put into words because these people are your safe place. They know the person you are, they know what you deserve and instead of you getting it, it seems like God gives it to them and leaves you out there to deal with it on your own. Oh and you gotta act happy so you don't look like a hater too lol. This strain will have you feeling like "I knew it was something wrong with me". This is literally the weirdest thing that will make you lose your mind especially if you don't handle that solitude properly. I had to understand the stain is not real, it's a part of the testimony, it's not who you are. You're not damaged goods, your process is just different. When you feel alone the most, that's when God can begin his work on you. Every emotion I talked about in this section I went through. God was exposing and stripping me of all these things that I didn't even know were there. That hurt manifested in my low self-esteem, it peaked when I wanted to become sexually active, it popped out in my friendships and relationships in abandonment issues and comparison. I'm not gonna tell anybody in this battle that it just goes away because as you are going through these cycles of growing and maturing, a new level of you will come to the surface. As long as you GET through the cycles and not just go through them, you will learn the things you need to learn to not have to go through them anymore. It was so much I needed to learn about myself and these cycles showed those things to me. Then God sat me by myself and made me sit with those very things that I thought made me a good person but instead, he revealed to me was coping mechanisms from hurt and trying to protect myself versus healing myself.

Love & Affection

They didn't tell us

How important affection is early on in our lives

The value of a two parent home

That strength can become toxic

The need for healthy relationships with both parents

As a child grows into an adult certain things should come naturally to them. Love and affection are two things that a child feels from the womb and should be even more once they come into the world. The love and affection of each parent is super important to the growth and development of the child. But often within families in this generation, the child is receiving these things from one parent while the other parent lives at a distance. Although co-parenting is such a popular thing, unless both parents are fully committed to building their relationship with the child, naturally at times, the child will begin to feel some sense of lack from the other parent. I have never been big on down talking my parents for anything they have ever done or not done in my life. The reason being is because at the end of the day I think I grew up to be a pretty dope woman. But the overall reality of life is I just did not come from an affectionate family. Now I am sure some people are going to read this and be like "man that's crazy" because I am very affectionate. But a lot of people do not understand that was a reaction to me getting lack thereof growing up.

Growing up in a single-parent home raised by three strong women I never needed much of anything. I always had a roof over my head, always had clothes on my back and food on the table. My Mother was always hustling making money, figuring out many ways of income. I can remember my mother doing hair, nails, and making decorative plants that people could put on their tables or hang on their walls. She was always grinding pushing to make sure I did not need anything. Whatever she did not do my grandmother surely took care of it. I was the oldest and only grandchild for 10 years before my little brother was born so it was not too many things that I could request without getting them. I am laying this visual for you because I need you to understand the dynamics of a lot of Mother-Daughter or parent-child relationships in African American Families. Before I go any further, I do need to say that I am not taking a jab at my mother's parenting. I had an amazing childhood growing up and I do not ever want her to feel as though I do not appreciate all of the things, she put into me. But while I was having that great childhood there were habits that I was picking up unknowingly. Watching my mother work and hustle and my grandmother also working as hard as they did instill a work ethic in me. Now I know again you are probably reading this like "well, what is wrong with that?", NOTHING... Nothing is wrong with gaining a work ethic. It is the other dynamics that come into play with that work ethic and the way I learned it that brought forth some problems. My father was an entrepreneur and my mother as I stated was a hustler with a 9 to 5 as well. My grandmother and Great Mothers were gamblers naturally. These were elements that I watched growing up mostly from women. My Mother, Grandmother, and Great Grandmother always made sure that things were taken care of. I do not remember having a strong male provider growing up, or even seeing a strong male figure period in my life until later. In this way, I saw women in that role. Women who would not allow for their children to know a struggle, so they worked their tails off to make sure the house was taken care of, and bills were paid. It was two things that I learned from these Strong Black Women that raised me.

- Strength
- Independence

The dynamics of my family and the way that the women in my family took the lead on everything, those two words can begin to grow into bad habits and personality flaws that need to be corrected as you grow into an adult. It was something that once I got older, I notice was completely absent within my family... Affection. I have a work ethic that I have from my mother and father, I have a mentality that I am always going to help my family no matter what from how my grandma and Great Grandma. I know how to buckle down and take care of business like my Auntie Vada, and I understand the value of Education like my Auntie Kathy. But for some reason, with inheriting all these great qualities when I would see my friends interacting with their mothers and how their mothers told them they loved them and always reassured them of them being there even for the smallest things, I would get this empty feeling in my stomach. So, I begin to investigate that feeling. I looked at how my mom interacted with my grandma and even the times my great-grandma was alive how she was with her children. That out in the open affection was just not there. I remember hugs being so awkward between myself and my mother and even my grandma as I got older. I remember when my mom told me she loved me before I went into surgery, she said it like a doorbell tune or something lol. I love yooou. Now it is funny to me as I write this, but I am being completely honest. I had grabbed all these work ethics and other things from all these strong women but my ability to show affection was nonexistent. Out of all my cousins growing up, I can say that I was the most sensitive and that of course did not change as I got older. I often found myself questioning God at a young age, even though I had no idea who he even truly was, but I questioned him and vividly remember being extremely mad that I was so sensitive. The smallest things made me cry, hurt my feelings, gave me that big empty feeling in the pit of my stomach. I want to point out that due to the fact I saw women in my family always putting on this strong front and doing what needed to be done, I truly thought something was wrong with me because I was so sensitive and showed uncontrollable emotions.

Mothers, especially single Mothers I need you to hear me and hear me loud and clear. We appreciate you. We are thankful that you have fed us, kept us clothed, kept a roof over our heads, and covered every need and want. We can not thank you enough for the late nights you spent in hospitals or driving all over the city taking us to practices after getting off work just as a means to try to keep us involved in productive things. But with all these things we need you to remember to love on us. We need you to remember that same way women preach that Fathers cannot substitute time spent with money, you cannot substitute your lack of Motherly affection with the things you provide. We need you to remember that the clothes do not heal that emptiness of not hearing "I love you" as often as we needed to when we were growing up. We need you to know you being open to listening when we make mistakes or fall versus trying to be disciplinary to supplement the other parent not being around, is not what we need all of the time. We need you to know that we need you to tell us that as a young woman it is ok to tell another woman that she is beautiful and wish the best for her. We need you to instill in us the values of being trustworthy and supportive. These are the things that will grow us into great friends. This type of affection is what will help us build lasting bonds with other women without letting bitterness and jealously creep in.

I know that in a world full of craziness and kids being exposed to things very prematurely it is a full-time job trying to keep your "Good Mama" persona up for the world. The pressures of a young woman who does not want to embarrass her mother are just as heavy to carry at times because that image becomes more important than the "Love". While you are teaching us to be strong and independent do not forget to teach those softer things. Honestly, the only way for you to teach them is to reflect them to us. The reason I say this is because it's not rocket science to know that as young women grow older, we start developing a mind of our own very quickly. It then becomes harder and harder for our parents to try to influence us during those teenage years. The problem with that is those years are usually the years where we make most of the mistakes that follow us into Adulthood. Then we spend the early part of our 20s trying to correct and now listen to the things that you were trying to tell us while we were growing. It is like racing against a clock at that point, so that is why the initial investment of Love and affection into us early on is so important. It is what will build our confidence, it is what will be the building of our foundation as a woman. We will not have to look at women on social media or fall into a million bad relationships for us to find out that we are beautifully and wonderfully made or that our home girl's light does not dim our own.

Father's, again especially single Fathers, the same way we need that affection from our mothers to kick start our development.... We need the same if not more from you. That whole saying that a father is the first example that a girl must have to show her how a man is supposed to treat her is BIG FACTS. I know sometimes circumstances do not allow for you to be in the child's life as much as you probably would like. But the time that you do have should be impactful. Again, I do not want either of my parents to feel as though I am attacking them in any form or fashion because at this point in my life I feel as though my relationship with my mom and dad is in a great place. My dad is a lot more affectionate than my mom and honestly, I think that is what has balanced me out. But it is still certain things that my dad just was not there for. Things that required HIS affection, him telling me I was beautiful and that my value was not in anyone else. I took relationships and commitment extremely seriously when I was young because that affection meant the world to me. So, trust me when I tell you, Fathers, we need you. We need your love; we need you to be a man of your word. We need to know that the small things in our lives matter to us.

One of my favorite Fathers in the world is my best friend Quell. When he had his daughter, I watched him completely change as a man. I watched how he talked to her. I watched him take his daughter on dates and take her to get her toes and nails done. I watched the gentleness come into his voice when he spoke to her. But I also watched her response when he was disciplining her and when she knew he was telling her something right to do. His correction was accepted in her life early because his affection had made a space for him in her heart. She knew when her father meant business and although her feelings may have been a little hurt during it, she took it because she knows her father loves her. She knows the lengths and the depths her father will go through for and with her. That is a love that can not be shaken and a foundation that when she learns from her mother how to be submissive to the man that God brings into her life, her father's affection will show her the type of man to recognize deserves that submission.

His relationship with his daughter will make her relationship and submission to God come with less strain as she gets older as well. For most people who struggle in faith, most of the struggle starts with submitting in the first place. But the word says "Train up a child in the way they should go and when they are old, they will not depart from it"- Proverbs 22:6. This is one of the situations I think of when I hear that. The things a parent plants in their child are the things that grow later in life. Things do not have to be directly spiritual to be beneficial in a child's spiritual growth. Each parent brings a different dynamic of what God intends for a child to learn. This point leads me to the next thing that God begins to reveal to me about my family dynamic and exposing the things that needed to be broken before starting the next generation. God showed me the value of the order. The word says, "But I want you to understand that the head of every man is Christ, the head of a wife is her husband, and the head of Christ is God"- 1 Corinthians 11:3. The man is the head and knowing the order that God ordained for things to go within this helpmate situation and in the family became all the more clearer for me while going through this revelation.

Again, throughout this book, I will speak my peace at moments out of respect for my friends and loved ones who may identify with different sexual orientations or different religions. I at no point intended to leave anyone out or try to press my ideas upon anyone. I am a believer in Love for all. God is Agape Love, so I have a love for all of those who love all and even the ones who do not. These are truly just my revelations from within my personal journey.

I do not care what anyone says, the value of a two-parent household has been watered down in this world and it should not be. A man and woman are helpmates to each other and watching women provide and take on the roles of men and then struggle to be in relationships with their kids are all too common. These same women also struggle to maintain healthy relationships with the opposite sex. Men and Women have different roles not only in life but in the process of raising children as well. A woman who must do EVERYTHING will have a hard time settling in a situation where the man is not bringing forth the same if not more. This can make a woman come off as Too Strong and overly independent and if we are being honest here that is a label that many black women carry today. Then stack that on top of a woman watching this happen for generations before her. Watching her mother and Grandmother provide, there is little room left for them to show affection to their children. Now you look up and you have a generational problem that has taken root just off these women doing what they feel like they MUST do.

"She does not need you, she got it! She has had it this long!" Men believe it or not sometimes that is a cry for help. Women are not built to carry that load alone; in fact, no one is. If you are carrying that load alone, I guarantee you are lacking in some other extremely important areas. When women are taking the lead and in control of everything the children miss out on that motherly affection. A woman working 12 hours, who has to go grocery shopping when she gets off, make sure the kids are clean and fed, keep herself up, make sure she has a sitter when the kids are not in school, and oh yeah make sure the kids are doing well in school (Or she's labeled a bad mom), sleep, and keep herself up; what does this woman have left to give her children? If a woman has that man or person who takes that strain of financial burdens and shares in the providing of a child that they have created together, it levels out the playing field. So many men think once they cut the check for child support that is enough. It's so much more to support a child than money. I know we have heard that before but think about when a single mother is dating and goes through a bad breakup. Emotionally she does not have time to deal with herself because her kids still need her at demand. A full-time single parent does not get a pause button even when that check hits the bank account.

The same goes for the men, if you have that helpmate you can be the provider and leader that you naturally desire to be. When men are solely focused on providing, they lack time spent as Fathers. Men are natural providers so in their heads when they have children that elevate their grind. They work more, they hustle more, and see the kids when they can. Unlike the mother or other parent who may have the child all the time, this parent determines when and how much they see the child. They may send money; they may pick the child up and take them shopping but that time of not being there is crucial. It is hard as a child to take discipline from a parent they do not see a lot. It is rough as a child when you are not getting the affection you desire and need for your development at home from one parent, then you must call the other parent and hope that they even answer the phone. So again, this puts all the weight back on one parent to be the provider and disciplinary. Overall, the child is receiving the short end of the stick on both ends. Then the child grows up and thinks this is how this goes, and the cycle just continues. I am not saying I have the solution to this problem because as individual people you come with your own issues into the relationship anyway. But if you have an area where you are lacking, your child has a 50/50 chance that the other parent can pick up where you lack. Now I know some people will read this and be like "Well what if we tried to stay together after having the kid and it just did not work?". Listen in most cases while you are in a relationship with a person you know exactly who that person is. Now if you choose to be blind to the flaws that is a personal choice. But within that choice, you must know some of those flaws will show the type of parent they will be.

This brings me back to my initial statement of God showing me the value of the order. MARRIAGE is a word that is key to me because in a marriage there is order. The principles of marriage and the intent of the commitment are what I believe are the foundation for the child. Now some people remain with their significant other without ever getting married and they work and both parents are in the house, this is rare, but it does happen. I am just speaking purely on the things God showed me during this time concerning family dynamic and why some of the things I thought were normal, were not. Take what you will from this but the revelation that God was giving me was why he set things the way he did as far as the balance needed to raise a child. I am not saying that marriage is the end-all-be-all solution. But what I am saying is for a little girl growing up who does not see the women in her life in healthy relationships does not even understand the purpose of marriage let alone the value of it. I think this was just God's way of teaching me by just using my own life and experiences as an example starting with the affection thing.

Lesson Learned

It was after learning these things about myself and the need for affection for a child that God showed me the value of Marriage and a two-parent household. Now again this is not something that I grew up seeing because marriage just is not a thing in my immediate family. Shoot I had not even seen any healthy relationships within my immediate family at this point. This revelation was important to me because it showed me something that I knew I did not want to carry on into the next generation. I knew I did not want to have children out of wedlock. I wanted to have that two-parent household established long before my child comes into the world. This would kick off my process of self-healing and deal with the things in me that needed to be dealt with before I ever even starting to seriously date. Knowing about the order was important but the key to this lesson was for me to understand that I needed to make some changes in myself. I knew what lacked between my mother and myself and then I realized it was not there because it lacked between her and my grandma and so and so forth. It is hard for us to expect something from our parents that they did not receive and honestly when we do not receive it that puts a strain on our relationship. Although the strains within myself and my mother and grandmother were not that bad, it was there, and I just knew the things as a mother that I didn't want to exhibit with my own child.

3

I ain't mad at you

They didn't tell us

Our parents were humans before and after they became our parents.

Sometimes we have to be the bigger person even if it's with our parents

Forgiveness is about you not the other person

Our healing is tied to the healing of our parents

Parents/ people can't give tools that they don't have.

I think my favorite part of my father and I's relationship is the fact that people see us now and will never know how this relationship actually started. It's a testament to God's grace and his ability to change the view of what people see. When he changes things he changes them so that no residue is left. I grew up raised by a single mother, grandmother, and great-grandmother, and not too many strong male influences around me. I Always knew who my father was. I just didn't have much of a relationship with him when I was younger. I can be honest because I've had these conversations with my dad. This realization in my life comes from me learning through the healing of our relationship that parents are human. He explained to me he just was very immature at the time when he decided to start having kids, simple as that. Now as a child it's not as simple as that but now that I'm an adult I understand it more than ever. The reality is In most cases immaturity is the case. Most people, not just men, are very immature until a child is brought into the picture. But again the reality is when we decide to have children early no matter what the Father decides to do the Mother has to mature at the moment they find out they are pregnant not just when the child gets here.

Not growing up with him definitely played a role in my personality growing up. I am a balance between my mother and my father. My mother is very hot-tempered and very sensitive but also very direct. She can come off as aggressive and angry at times but she has great intentions. My father on the other hand is very calm, he doesn't think too much with his emotions but with logic for the most part, and extremely charming. I'm very calm-natured. I was very quiet growing up but I paid attention and internalized everything. I remember my first time reading "I Know Why the Caged Bird Sings" by Maya Angelou. I found myself almost fully in the imagination of the main character of the book. The main character "Maya went through trauma as a child and once she told her family what happened to her the person who hurt her ended up dead. She then stopped talking because she thought her words had killed the man. During the time of her not talking to people, she was taking in everything so when she finally was ready to talk again, she had something to say. I often feel like that's a reflection of my life in more ways than one. Now that I'm older I can definitely feel myself opening up more about the things I saw and experienced growing up, with more clarity. I feel as though I'm able to express how I was processing my life then compared to now. I realized I internalized a lot of things and put them in these little compartments of my mind until I could make sense of them.

I'm saying all this to say that I went through the normal phase as a child who does not grow up with her father. I thought I didn't need him because my mom and grandma did everything. As normal as a lot of us think that is, it's not. In fact, as a child, you should not be deprived of either parent because you literally need both to teach you the way of life from their natural perspectives. I went from not really knowing who he was, as in a relationship, to knowing him but still being so angry I didn't care to know him. Then I knew I needed him even with the strong male influences I started to have in my life as I got older. I knew what he looked like, I knew he looked like me, I knew I had curly hair like him and I knew he had a mom I looked like. I also knew I had siblings. I had never met the siblings and as a child, at this point, you don't know the backstory of anything that's happening in your life.

I don't remember ever hearing my mom cursing my dad out and telling him he can't see me. But I do remember days where my mom was supposed to meet him to drop me off to spend time with him or times he was supposed to come to get me and he didn't come. Those were days where I saw mama call and trip out. It wasn't her trying to keep me away from him, it was her being upset that he wasn't trying to be near me. Then I remember getting to a point where I didn't really hear from him or talk to him much. It was also around this time I began to discover my love for basketball. So that is where I started to put a lot of my negative energy.

My initial fuel to keep getting better was to deal with internal anger. I wasn't the lash-out person or do bad stuff to get my parent's attention but I was very much aware of my emotions at a very early age. I didn't know not having my dad around would affect me at the core of my development as much as it did. I found myself in a lot of situations at a very young age that I probably shouldn't have been but those are things that can happen when you have a young girl growing up looking for her identity in people. That unbalance in the home will always reveal itself in the child if the co-parent situation is not healthy. Single Mothers are providers and household managers, so it's hard to emotionally be present. Father's when you are not emotionally present and physically absent your child in most cases is going to spend much of her life looking for that in other males. I've had conversations with my older cousin Brittney and we can definitely agree to the extent that although we did not have a terrible childhood there are a lot of things that we just weren't aware of that would impact our future as much as it did. One of the things we realized was it's hard to demand something from a parent that they may not have received from their own parents, to begin with. This realization opened my eyes to a lot of possibilities as to why my dad was the type of dad he was. This gave me a soft spot for him. Not soft enough for me to not be mad at him at that point in my life but soft enough for me to leave that space open for us to deal with our issues at some point in time.

My dad wasn't around much but then it changed and he started coming to get me more and coming to my games. I remember he used to work at Footlocker or FootAction and I would pop in to go see him when I would need shoes or just to see him. But then my grandmother passed away, his mother. I went to the funeral and this is where I was able to meet my siblings as well as a lot of my father's side of the family. I remember after the funeral I was able to just hang around my sisters and brother. I was extremely standoffish because I just didn't feel like I knew anybody and that is an interesting place to be in as a child to come around your family you don't know and somehow or another you have to find a way to be comfortable in a setting that should've been comfortable from the beginning. After the funeral, I was able to spend a lot more time with my dad because he would have me and my sisters and my brother over to visit. At the time he had a girlfriend named Lisa I believe, she would do pedicures and stuff for us. I remember I had a project for school and my uncle David and Adrian are both extremely talented but my uncle David can draw and he drew a Tiger for me, a white tiger. Those are a lot of my earlier memories of being around my dad and my siblings. But it's crazy now because even with remembering those times I still don't remember us actually having a relationship like I just remember being at his house I don't necessarily remember talking or anything like that to my dad. I remember going to our family reunion and this was my first time being around this much and I remember him getting up and speaking and talking about him being able to mend our relationship and spend more time with me, me pretty much me being the long lost child and all. This time of my life was very bittersweet because as I said it was great I was good and bonding with my siblings but still didn't necessarily have a bond with my dad and it was so much going on in my life at that age and I just felt like I really needed him and I just didn't know how to communicate that. At the time I'm like nine or 10 years old and as I've said I've always had a hard time communicating out of the thought that I could potentially lose the person by saying something wrong. The crazy thing is this is my father. How can I lose someone who is my parent? But that's how I felt, plus I was just enjoying being around him so I was pretty much like I'll take what I can get and keep it moving.

Next thing we know my dad is getting married. I'm still able to spend time a little bit more with my siblings then I also now have two stepbrothers, a younger and older one to add to the bunch. Even with spending more time over my dad's at this point after he was settled in his new home with his new wife and family, I still just always felt out of place when I would visit. My sisters and brother were over a lot more so they spent more time and built stronger bonds with our new brothers and because my visits had so many gaps in between I always felt like I was starting over when I came back around. But then our house caught on fire. After the fire, I went and stayed with my dad for like a week to make sure I could get back and forth to school. So this gave me a little bit more time to be around everyone and kind of start getting a little bit more comfortable. My dad was coaching at this time so we were starting to connect in another area as far as basketball is concerned as well. But as we got close I started to realize how involved my father was in the kids' lives he was coaching. That honestly made me feel some type of way because I was playing the same sport he was coaching and here he was being this great mentor to these kids but I wanted him to be that to me as well. I couldn't understand how you could be this great role model and take these boys camping and do all these great things to help them bond when you and your own kids rarely went and did things with you altogether. At least that was my view of it.

It's funny now because Facebook has a bad habit of reminding you of when you were extremely immature lol. I often see statues in the past that I know were directly aimed at my dad. I remember telling myself I didn't need him. I wanted to hate this man so bad y'all. But God just did not make my heart that way and I am extremely happy that he didn't. No matter how upset I was, I couldn't hide the smile I got when he came around. I couldn't hide the pride I got when people told me how much I looked like him. But at this point in my life, which is like middle school and high school I wasn't really sure what more our relationship could grow into. Although he was showing up to big events more it wasn't enough for me. I wanted him to make up for the time in the past. I wanted him to take me out and it was just me and him. I wanted to know why he didn't stay with my mom. I wanted to tell him what dudes who had no business touching me had done to me. I wanted to know why he only felt like keeping the other 3 kids close to him was important. I wanted him to know how empty I felt around his family because I didn't know them. I wanted to tell him how mad I was that he held up my siblings' and I's relationship. I honestly didn't know how much anger I had built up towards this "MAN" until recently in the last couple of years when God was healing me. The word man is standing out here for a reason. Before I finish my story here and start heading in the direction of telling how God began to shift this situation, I have to mention that God has always told us to never put our trust in man. I need us to know that this doesn't exempt our parents. I'm not negatively saying this I'm saying it to show the start of me realizing my father was just that... a **MAN**.

Now I have gotten through high school. I had done two years of college here and over those years my dad was definitely starting to be a lot more active in my life. But again I still felt like our relationship had these holes in it that I didn't think was my job to fill and honestly I thought the way our relationship was at that point was exactly the way it would be. When I'm around him we were good and when I wasn't it was whatever. Sometimes we go weeks without talking and that would be that. He came to all my college home games, I started being around my family more, it was a decent healthy space to be in but I still had this anger that I couldn't put into words about our crippled past. I did exactly what I always do which was not say anything, suffer in silence and just try to keep it moving. Because although I couldn't tell my dad how I felt at least he was in my life right?

But then something happened. I moved away in the midst of my dad going through a divorce. I left to go to college in Tennessee and me and my dad began to talk more than we ever did. Not more in the sense of amount but more in substance. Our conversations were long and included a variety of subjects from sports and the game from a player standpoint vs. a coach's. He would even share with me his ideas about future business endeavors. But one day he called and I could hear the stress in his voice. My dad was hurting, he had moved to Virginia in hopes of making his marriage work and ultimately it just didn't. What I found interesting about this convo was that my dad was at a level of vulnerability that not only had I never seen from him but that I had never seen from a man in my life. He was hurt, disappointed in himself, beaten down, and also spread thin because at the time my second oldest sister was battling newly diagnosed Lupus. She and my oldest sister were either preparing to have their first child or they were already here I can't remember. I saw him upset about his failure of being able to be a husband but also his hurt of not being able to be a hands-on father and grandfather during my sister's transitions into Motherhood. Talk about being human! This was like seeing a superhero be stripped of their powers for that short period of time in a movie. This was my first time with the thought like wow my dad is really a human, a man. He has feelings like I do, he stumbles as I do. The conversation was the beginning of God taking the veil off my eyes. I no longer saw him as my dad, the man who shouldn't do any wrong because you are an adult and you made adult decisions to have kids so you shouldn't be moving the way you are. Now I was seeing him as just a human who probably went through some things in his life like I did that made him that way. The same issues I had with him it was very well possible that he had some as well. See sometimes we can be so blinded by our own trauma and pain that we can't see what God may actually be doing in the midst of it. Our natural view of a situation has the potential to hold up the things in movement spiritually if we can't get over what we see or how we feel in the moment. I could've easily stayed in my feelings about whatever happened in the past and that could have stopped this conversation with my dad from ever happening. Me deciding although I had my own issues with my dad to keep leaving that door open allowed me to begin to see firsthand God move. My whole visual of my father changed after that and I began to feel a love for him that was deep. Not a daddy's girl love but a love of compassion for whoever that little boy was in him that was still growing and trying to figure things out while dealing with himself on a daily.

THIS IS THE MOVE

While in my last semester of school God started placing on my heart that I needed to move back home. Now let's be clear I had NO intentions of moving back home after graduation. But I also knew that this wasn't the first time me and God were on two completely different pages. I began dealing with really bad migraines and eventually was diagnosed with a broken nose and nasal passages that needed to be ballooned. This made the decision to go home make more sense because I knew I would have to have surgery and knew it would make my mom and grandma more comfortable if I was home. I also at this time was beginning to discover a new passion in myself with speaking and being involved with the youth, this lead to me having the desire to start a mentoring program back home. While I thought God was pulling me home so that I could thrive and do his work lol. What I didn't know was that you can't actually do God's work or walk into your calling carrying certain things in your heart... one of those things being unforgiveness. Jesus walked with the worst of the worst but no matter what they knew they had to carry themselves a certain way when it came to doing his work. No matter what your life may look like, your heart can't be a mess and that's what he was targeting when I was getting ready to come home. Sure enough, he would reveal my purpose to me but not without work being done to get me there first.

When I got back home my dad got me a job to work at a school with him. At the time he was working as a para at Michigan collegiate high school. Originally he pushed to get me in the school to coach, the job in the school was just supposed to be for me to have some type of income starting. But I really didn't want to coach at the time but I needed the money so I went on with the plan. I agreed to be the coach for middle school girls and to help find a high school coach for the girls. I would assist with the high school girls but I just didn't feel like I was ready to coach high school yet. When I got to Michigan my health began to deteriorate a little bit more. I started passing out whenever I would get these very painful headaches throughout my day. It started happening so much to the point that my mom and my grandmother forbid me from driving. Then not long before I started work, my car stopped working. So this led my father to come to get me for work every day. What I need you all to understand is that my dad lives deep west and I lived deep east. The school was on 13 mile and Ryan which is heading north and is kind of like in the middle of both of us. So my dad would have to ride past the school to come to get me and then drive us to the school. Now I didn't think about how much of a sacrifice that had to be until literally just now but when I tell you all the joy I got out of our conversations from us driving to school every day it's unexplainable.

As I've said, one of my biggest issues with me and my father's relationship is I felt like I didn't know him and he didn't know me. This time in the car together it put us in a position where we didn't have a choice but to get to know each other because we had to ride to work every single day together. So during this time, we were having conversations about music and about emotions and relationships, just all sorts of things that really opened up my mind to his mind. It showed me how he thinks and the things that he likes and the things that we had in common. This went on for a while and honestly, I think it laid the foundation for me to feel so comfortable talking to my dad about things that were uncomfortable to talk about. So this goes on for at least the first year my dad came and got me every day even if he didn't take me home he came and got me every day and that time we talked and we grew and the more time we spent together at the school we grew in our professions as well. I also joined his coaching staff as an assistant coach for the boy's team so I spent more time with him strategizing and helping him not only grow as a coach because I'm giving him the mind of a player but also he was pouring into me as well as a coach. I spent more time with my dad in that year than I've ever had in my whole life. And it literally started to transform our relationship from that point forward.

To take some stress off of my dad from him having to drive all the way east, some days I would stay the night at his house so that I would already be there and he wouldn't have to drive to my side of town for work. One particular week I had been listening to the song by Kierra Sheard called "Free". I listened to this song a gazillion times in a week and God began to speak to me and all he would say was "be free". Now I've been very open about the trauma that I've dealt with in my life and just my learning process of how to get through it, but I have never been honest with somebody this close let alone a parent with what I had gone through in my life. Honestly, there's some stuff that I had just decided that I would deal with between me and God and I would just take it to my grave but God told me "No". So this day I had listened to it the night before and I could hear God loud and clear saying "Be Free". It was becoming overwhelming how loud God was speaking to me. So we got in the car and as we got to about 696 freeway I looked over and I said "Daddy, I got to tell you something but I need you to promise me that you are not gonna cry". He looked at me and said: "oh boy". I told him he couldn't cry but I had to say it because God was telling me I had to, he said "OK". I said daddy "I was molested when I was a kid and for so many years I've blamed you or I was so angry with you for not being in my life because I felt like if you were around that wouldn't have happened to me".

As a father you are my first line of defense, you're my first line of protection and not only were you not there to protect me you just weren't there. Because my mom had to play both mom and dad that took her away to provide for me. Not saying that they just left me with anybody but in this particular situation, but I felt like had you protected me it wouldn't have happened initially. Now the continuance of the act over the years from a completely different person again I still blamed you. I blamed you because had you taught me what love was like and been affectionate and been in my life I would've known that this was wrong. I would know what the proper love and affection from a male is supposed to look like and I would've been able to defend myself properly in the situations or even be able to express myself better.

I said "Daddy for so many years I've been so mad at you and I couldn't say it but I don't want to be mad anymore. I love you and I know that everything that happened while I was young was just a result of you and my mother being young. I had to let this go because I've carried this pain in my soul for so long and I don't wanna carry it anymore". Well, I could tell y'all that He did pretty well, my dad didn't cry, which I was extremely surprised about LOL. But we got through that moment and my dad looked at me and we had probably one of the hardest conversations I've ever had in my life but my dad gave me some history on him and his growing up in the conversation and that key opened up a chapter of me. It showed me a part of me that I never understood. This was very much my first understanding of generational curses. Not saying that my dad had the same experience as me but certain traumas come through a bloodline and you don't understand it at that moment because you're so young. My father started to talk to me and I understood his troubles with his father and literally the reflection of his life with his father was dang near the same as me and his. So this is where generational curses and trauma became very real to me. This showed me how one cannot parent if one does not deal with the things that their parents didn't deal with while parenting them. (Pruning is part of the promotion process)

I will always consider myself a good person and I knew very early on that I was different because I was so sensitive and things bothered me emotionally on a very high level. I didn't understand it until later but having that very transparent conversation with my father that day showed I have a lot of characteristics of him. Crazy thing is my strength, the person that I am comes from those experiences so being able to be transparent with the person that I felt hurt me the most in my life and is responsible for a lot of the pain that I carried around it opened a door for me. Open to the point I hadn't been able to truly allow myself to be open in any relationship with another male and I truly didn't understand why. I just thought it was because I was a focused young lady and I was always focused on my goals and accomplishing the things that I had at hand which was probably true to an extent. But I also was very reserved in being able to fully give myself to somebody just based of the fact that I didn't trust people men particularly. A lot of us carry around abandonment issues and we don't realize that they manifest in other areas of our lives. We may just think "I'm a strong black woman I don't have time for foolishness" is really how we feel. In all honesty you are not even open enough to allow somebody to get close to you. I'm a very self-reflective person but it took me until this moment and being able to talk to my father to actually see I had a wound that I didn't deal with concerning my own father. So once I healed from that and was able to finally communicate those feelings and let the anger out, I honestly feel more ready for a relationship now than I ever have in my life.

Lessons Learned

Parents are human at the end of the day. We cannot let the issues that we have as we grow into young adults bleed over into other areas of our lives. In most cases whatever our parents are struggling with stems from something they didn't get from their own parents or childhood. So we have to extend that same amount of grace that we would want somebody to extend to us or that we want to extend to our own child, to our own parents. We have to understand that they were growing and making mistakes based on their circumstances and we just don't know what their circumstances were at that time. But we do know if they were still kids and we know this because at this point in our lives we have lived the age that they were when we came into this world. I couldn't imagine being 19-20 years old with a kid like my mom. That's a woman, now we're supposed to mature sooner right? Now I have to imagine my father, who had multiple kids young. That maturity just is not there and I have to give that Grace to that part of my Father. Be clear in the fact that during the growing process mistakes happen people are not perfect and we have to remove our parents in particular from this pedestal once we get to a certain age so that we can truly not only mend our relationship with them but for us to be better parents. This is so we don't carry that anger into our parenting because it's going to alter your vision on certain things. Ultimately that could affect your relationship with your child in ways that you won't even understand because you won't understand that you're doing certain things, certain ways because of hurt. I don't want to parent out of hurt, I want to parent out of love.

I also learned that forgiveness is not for the other person, forgiveness is for you. We have to be able to move past something that bothers us to get us in a better headspace and more productive space. Sometimes you can hold a grudge towards somebody or something and It'll be so strong that you can't be productive. If I continued to carry around unforgiveness for my father I wouldn't be productive in relationships. I wouldn't be productive when it came to dealing with male authority figures. This was something that I realized about him once I made a decision that I was OK. I didn't grow up in a bad life or without because he wasn't in my life. So now I just wanted to start from where we were and go from that point, regardless of him being in my life or not at one point, I'm OK.

This situation also opened my eyes for him to parent me now. Growing up my mom and my grandma, my great-grandma had to be the authority figures. So with all of those hats as I said earlier that's when she was doing all the parenting. She was the one making sure my work for school was done. I feel like my mother parented me into adulthood and now in adulthood, I need my father more. In my Mother's eyes, I'm always her child, I'm her baby, any problem I have she wanna fix it, etc. With my dad, he wasn't there for that time so now he's able to parent me without the biased view. He can parent me as an adult and not his baby. He gives me a choice and direction that he wishes he would have got at this time of his life. That balance is so necessary because, without it, my mother's help can become a crutch. Because no matter what I know she's there parenting me her way, the way she knows. If I fall, my Mother is going to pick me up. She may be cussing me out while she picks me up, but she is going to pick me up. I need those two different angles and perspectives. It's the perfect combo, in my opinion, it's that perfect combo of parenting that has grown both relationships with both my parents.

The last thing I learned was as a child you have to sometimes be the bigger person. You have to be the one who makes the decisions that may mend your relationship. The thing with me and my father's relationship is I thank God that my mother allowed me to see who my father was on my own. She didn't down-talk my father, she didn't belittle him in front of me. She allowed me to go through my process. When I was old enough to understand what was going on or what wasn't going on she just let me go through it. She let me see who he was for myself and come to my own conclusions. Now with coming to those conclusions, I went through many phases of being angry at him but now at this point, I can't imagine him not being as active in my life as he is now. I decided that once I pretty much re-met my father I was going to accept him for whatever he was at that time. I wanted him in my life so I needed our relationship to work and that was me being the understanding one. We always come into the situation thinking "why do I have to fix the relationship with you", "Why do I have to be the one to build this relationship when I didn't ask to be here". I understand this but at a certain point, Ima just say you could be the key to the next phase of your healing and the next phase of the next generation's healing. I move the way I move because I have nieces and nephews in this world. I pray to have children of my own one day so I move in the manner of them not having to carry baggage from a generation that they are not even a part of.

When my father and I went through our healing situation, I was finally able to express to him the things that I was struggling with. Things that I dealt with growing up and things I blamed him for, when I was able to lay all that out to him we started our healing in our relationship blossomed from that moment. A couple of months after we went through this process my father lost his father. Now I had never met him and he had only met a few times in his life and had no relationship with him. So literally we turned around and we're in the same situation I was in as a child with me and my siblings. He met his siblings at his Father's funeral. My father was able to not only build relationships with these extended siblings but I think being able to go to this funeral and discovering that part of himself helped him heal as well. I definitely think the two were connected and I think the connection for those generational wounds was very important for the generations after. I am extremely grateful for the will and mind that God gave me to get through this experience because I know he's using me to move my family forward and I don't see a better honor.

4

It's Personal

They didn't tell us

Your connection with God is relational, not religious.

Deliverance is daily

Our Faith is like a muscle

Faith and works go together

Trials and Tribulation (You keep on keeping me)

Nobody tells you when you were growing up in a church that your relationship with God is personal. It's not built on what somebody tells you. It's not Built on even what you see so because when you are in church and you see these people hollering and praising and then go talk about somebody as soon as they take three steps out of the sanctuary that can shake the foundation of your faith before it ever really is established. If you are going into a building with the expectation that these people are gonna be 100 % the reflection of a Perfect God You can find yourself tainted and confused very early. When you grow up they teach you sanctification as a form of pretty much bullying you into religion. They tell you what you can and can't do but no lessons behind why you shouldn't. The connection of real-life to the bible is just not there when you are young and most older people have a hard time helping with that connection without coming off judgmental or preachy. It feels like most kids are being strong-armed into correction versus naturally going through the process. People encourage changed behavior but not changing of the heart. So that misconception can make you feel unworthy before you even truly know who God is for yourself.

When individuals are starting in their faith they are babes.. just like a young child being raised in the world. Children have very high spiritual radars when it comes to people and the energy they project. When a child is around a person and doesn't wanna be held by them or shows discomfort when they are around, or even cries when they try to hold them or interact with them, pay attention. That child if constantly put in that situation displays discomfort it's because they feel something off with that person. Children have an untampered conscience and no filter on the way they see life. They see it in the rawest form because they haven't seen any actual experiences yet. Nothing is there to cloud the child's judgment because they have no judgment at the moment. They are making those judgments based on how people make them feel. This is literally the same situation as young people or people in general who are starting fresh in their faith. They are babes in this world so their spirit is very sensitive even if they don't understand why. So when they are in an environment of the church and noticing the messiness, or feel uncomfortable it is in most cases because their spirit is not sitting well with those they have come in contact with. The word says "Try the spirit by the spirit" that doesn't only apply to people who are already in the church. This is how we get those negative reactions and perceptions that our youth come to about the church. They haven't experienced God enough for them to be strong enough to ignore the foolishness that may be going on so they result to retreating and create this false narrative of what the church is and what it should stand for.

Newborn- Growing up in the church, getting away from it

So first things first I grew up in the church. I was raised in the church. My aunt took me and my cousin Britney, to church every Sunday. Bible study was every Wednesday, we were doing all of that. Eventually, I got to a point as I got older where I started questioning the things that I was seeing in the church. I got baptized at about nine I believe. Truthfully at the time my cousin Britney was so influential in my development I did it because she did it. She got baptized so I said I didn't truly know God for myself and followed her lead. I didn't truly even have an actual awareness of God at that age. I was going to kiddie church and dealing with all these different attitudes. I didn't really like my Sunday school teacher. I think it's your responsibility as an adult teacher in the room to make every child feel comfortable and I just didn't get that so of course, it was hard for me to learn anything in Bible school. Eventually the older I got the more messy church began to be to me so I started to go less and less. Not even so much just with the messiness, my life was changing. I was becoming more involved with basketball and it was taking me away on weekends. My coach believed in practicing seven days a week so by the time I got to high school I just didn't have the time to go to church. At the time I was fine with it, I went through most of my high school years and I did not go to church at all other than funerals. I didn't even go for holidays like Easter and Christmas,

Let me make a disclaimer that at a very young age I knew when God was talking to me. I didn't know what to do with those thoughts a lot of times. I actually thought I was crazy a lot and I just never really said anything to anybody but I knew it when he would tell me things. Although I hadn't been in church in a while I was very sensitive in spirit. Basketball became the thing that came and took over my life. The saying that God is a jealous God is very much true and I honestly think in this situation he just wiggled his way into the thing that he knew had my attention the most. With basketball, he began to reveal himself through experiences but also people. I could lie right here and say that basketball pulled me away from church but the truth of the matter is I was extremely uncomfortable in the place I should have felt the most comfortable. I rarely talked and I would always get this guarded feeling whenever I would step into the building. I just honestly felt like everybody was being fake and that feeling became extremely overwhelming as a child and I just didn't wanna feel like I was being forced to conform and be fake once I got in that atmosphere. At this age, I knew I needed God. I just didn't know in what context and I wasn't gonna know because I wasn't about to keep going there lol.

This was my first exposure to understanding that this relationship could be more than what the church had to offer, in fact that it would be more than what the church had to offer. God showed me that he didn't need a building to get to me. He could use anything and anybody. At this particular point, he showed me through people. See if people are carriers of his light, they reflect exactly what it is he wants you to see. Him. Through their conversations, through their guidance, through their mistakes and failures, and even though their personal walks. God knew I wasn't gonna step back into a church for years to come. So he came to me. He met me right where I was, right where I wanted to be and he began to move.

Toddler- Spiritual crutches

When a child begins to learn to walk, that is a visual representation of the child moving into the toddler phase of their growth. This is the beginning of their independence and usually, the start of them starting to get their hands in a lot more things than they did before. Again this is the same for us at a certain point in our faith. We find ourselves in some of the most interesting situations while we are on this walk. But just like our parents are there when we fall to pick us up, God sends people who do the same. These people are a reflection of what I'm gonna say are crutches. The reason I am going to compare these people to crutches is that the reality of crutches is they are there for support during your time of trying to build your strength up, developing your balance, and ultimately for stability while you are trying to figure out how to walk again usually after an injury. Crutches are not meant to be permanent. In fact, if you are on them too long they can start hurting you instead of helping. Knowing when to let the crutches go, knowing when they have served as enough support and when it's time for you to put some pressure on is key to your healing and growth. If you don't start putting the pressure on you'll never learn to walk without that support.

Angel #1

When God sends people you know are his people his light is very evident in them and the way they come into your life and in the way that they stay. Your value for these people is gonna be a lot higher than some of your other relationships from your past. These people can come in the form of spouses, best friends, or even relatives but knowing How to value these people and how to properly engage with them is key to the things that God is going to bring forth through the relationship between you and them.

I was in high school heading into my Senior year. A little light skin girl whose mom started bringing her to our games started to imprint herself on my life. I'm going to refer to her as Angel number one. Eventually, we found out she was coming to the school to play ball. At the time we were having an undefeated season we ended up losing the district that year and when my senior year came Angel #1 transferred in from Cass Tech. Instantly when she joined the team we bonded and the fact she was post player meant my coach required us to spend a lot of time together on the court and then he asked me to take her under my wing off the court. I pretty much was mentoring her and then the friendship grew into a friendship outside of basketball. I think I took a liking to her because she was not like the rest of us. She didn't listen to rap music, she didn't even have her ears pierced. I'm talking about a whole church girl and she just seemed so quiet and innocent. Eventually that all would change and unfortunately I would like to say I had a lot to do with that corruption. But in the midst of my corrupting this young girl begins to pour into me spiritually.

See angel number one was young but she was raised in the church. She was raised by Godly women. She was very strong in her faith at a very young age. Now at this time, I've been out of church for some years and the saying try the spirit by the spirit is very real because as I said I was very sensitive spiritually even with me not really being in church. My spirit automatically gravitated to her. Although I would grow to be what she called her big sister she doesn't know she became a big sister to me a lot sooner than I became one to her. I personally considered being a big sister as picking them up, sneaking them to go see their boyfriends, introducing them to certain songs and teaching them about the songs, and giving them an safe place to talk and be themselves. Those were the elements that I viewed as being the older sibling and that's what I prided myself on being to them. But Angel #1 talked to me about the Holy Spirit, She talked to me about Prayer, She talked to me about fasting, She talked to me about Marriage and the values of marriage. Those are things that I just didn't see growing up because Marriage just wasn't a thing in my family. I remember going around her grandmother for the first time and her grandmother told a story of how she met her grandfather and she would always say "pay attention to how he treats kids". "Look at how kids respond to him". It was these types of engagements with her and her family and her spiritual side that began to light something in me again.

Eventually, Angel #1 started inviting me to church and for some reason, I just never really got around to it at first. I think the first time I went to church I took my cousin Brittney. She invited me and we had an amazing time and I was hooked after that. I think Pastor Dorian was preaching; he was young and relatable and I fell in love with the atmosphere of the church. So her speaking the things that she was speaking to me and her being completely honest about her walk begin to inspire me and that's what made me want to keep going to church even with the foolishness I was teaching them. It was kind of like an exchange, I was making her a little bit more worldly and she was pulling me in spiritually.

Watching Angel #1 be so bold in her walk even when we were so in our worldliness, even through us cracking jokes on her, she was so strong in who she was that inspired me. I remember going through my first Bible series with her and just the things that she would talk to me about especially when I didn't understand something that fed me. This was who I went to for questions about the Holy Spirit. This is who I went to when I felt weak spiritually or when I wanted to know anything that pertained to my faith. When I needed explanations or anything I called on her. Keep in mind she's younger than me so this is proof that God will use anybody and anything to get to you. I'm not sure Angel #1 had the most enjoyable basketball experience there but I truly do not believe she was there for basketball. I can remember when she told me she wanted Tarry for the Holy Spirit. Now I had no clue what she was talking about. I just act as I did. I remember her telling me she went to church. She told her mom she wanted Tarry for the Holy Spirit. They took her to the back room and she told me the whole experience and I remember being terrified when she told me how this process went. I think I was terrified because growing up in a Baptist church you think The Holy Spirit is something that you get when you get old. So here it is, a little 16-year-old is telling me she spoke in tongues and she just wanna listen to gospel music for the next two weeks in her car and I'm trying to listen to some Wale. I watched her walk boldly into that and walk out boldly and be willing to talk about it just like you talk to someone about a new pair of shoes. I depended on her so heavily. She had gone to another level and I was excited for her but now I needed her to show me how to get to that place! At least that's what I thought.

When I got hurt in college she was the number one person I called when I needed prayer. When I was dealing with the dreams and tormenting nightmares about being molested, Angel #1 would answer that phone and she would pray for me three or 4 a.m. This young woman was a rock for me when I couldn't be one for myself. Most people reading this would agree that it is absolutely amazing to have a friend like that. This was a true testament to the person she is and most importantly the friend she is. But the same way I accepted her maturity spiritually I had to acknowledge her immaturity as well and at the time that was hard to do because I couldn't see past what I thought I needed from her. She was light, God put her in my life to teach me and guide me right? Big WRONG.

If at this point I can give any encouragement to young people it would be, know that you are never too young for God to use you. You are never too young for your life to reflect God and his grace for people or his love for people. All of these things were great because this is who she was to me. A reflection of Him. A teacher. But also in being this to other people you have to know when your cup needs to be refilled or filled to begin with. You have to know that you are a carry of the light you are not the light, you can't save people. As full as she was in my eyes, the reality was she was still young herself in her own faith. This can be compared to a child birthing a child. Becoming a young Mother while you are still developing as a child yourself rushes you into "maturity" a lot sooner than expected and with that comes a lot of mistakes.

But even through those mistakes the child's needs never stop. The child doesn't know that you were too young when you had it. All that child knows is I need you because you are where my source of comfort comes from, you are my connection. My crutch, That's what our friendship became. I say this because in the midst of all this good she was doing for me I missed the whole point of why God placed her in my life. When he sends a vessel his intent is not for you to begin to worship or depend solely on that vessel. The vessel is to teach something important to you and you are to take those things and grow and be able to turn around and do the same thing to somebody else. This is the overall message of Christianity. So many times we get so caught up in the building and not understanding that the building of who God is, the structure of him is in you.

No matter where she felt she was in her walk her light shined enough for me to see it. Enough to even help me light my own light. I began my walk again not because I got strong-armed, it was because of who he was in her. I saw a light and I wanted to get to wherever it was. I wanted whatever she was getting from this God she spoke so highly of and that I saw move in her life. But even with her light, I wouldn't be prepared for what God was about to do next.

After I got hurt it seemed like all my friends and the people that I had taken under my wing were passing me up. They were going to college on full scholarships, playing basketball, and thriving. Meanwhile, I was sitting at home in a knee brace. When I finally got out of the brace and I was able to go to Wayne County and things started progressing. But me and Angel #1's relationship started to deteriorate. We didn't talk as much. She was living in Indiana and she was in a full-blown committed long-distance relationship. I was losing my best friend not only to another state but to this other person at least that's what it felt like. She began to act a little weird to me at the time and I couldn't put my finger on it but it just was weird. Eventually, it got to a point where we didn't talk at all and that was absolutely not normal because we literally used to talk every day so I was struggling with that because this somebody who meant a lot to me and this is somebody who had poured into me and I just didn't understand what I had done to her. I had so many friends just kind of up and walk out of my life I was scared and just knew that's what was happening and I just remember praying like God if was the end of our friendship then I have to just accept your will. I literally laugh reading this because I was so dramatic. But I felt that deep and I just wanted to figure out how to move forward without this person that I just knew he had sent.

I eventually got a scholarship to Cumberland University in Lebanon Tennessee and I just thought that was the end of our friendship. While I was dealing with the process of losing a best friend and also walking through a kind of heartbreak, I found myself falling into a place of depression. It was in this place that God asked a question, he asked me did my relationship with him depend on Angel #1? Of course, I'm like "No God that wasn't the case she just helped me get back to you", but on the other side of that, He knew the truth. He knew I was depending on her to explain scripture to me instead of asking him for understanding. He knew I waited until I was with her to even talk to him or want to talk about him and that wasn't it. The introduction should have been just that and I should have taken that and ran right to him. Later on, as my faith began to grow during my time of being away and in Tennessee, me and Angel #1 begin to talk again. I remember one day we were talking and she said, "I feel like I finally can tell you this because I think you are maturing in the way that God saw fit". This was a random conversation. I don't even think we were talking about anything spiritually. We were just kind of catching up and she came out of the blue and said "God told me I had to separate myself from you". She said, "he didn't tell me why he just told me I needed to separate myself from you". After she said that we started kind of putting a puzzle together and this was the understanding that I got from the whole situation. I was depending too much on Angel #1 spiritually and not standing on my own two feet the way that God intended. See when a parent is teaching a child how to walk they might start with the kid standing on their feet or standing behind the child holding them up for balance. But the reality of walking is eventually the child has to learn to use their own weight and walk for themselves. If you constantly always walk with a child on your feet and their feet don't touch the ground how will they know how to maneuver through the rocks and bumps of their own paths. This understanding of the flaws in my perception showed me that my spiritual life had been reached a new level but also that my and Angel #1's friendship reached a different level as well. The love that I have for her for listening to God superseded any anger or anything that I have felt in the past because I knew she truly cared about me and I knew it hurt her just as much to completely remove herself from my life but her trust in God overruled that hurt.

Angel #2

Now with my relocating to Tennessee incomes Angel #2. I would've never thought my first time meeting this person that our friendship would grow to be what it is now. From our first dinner with her and the other coaches to just having regular conversations, to going through injuries and her being my source of comfort because I was away from my family, Angel #2 began to reflect what I always wanted in an older sibling. Now I am coming out of a situation where I was the big sister and my little sister was pouring into me to now that I'm in a different phase of my life and an older person is providing me with guidance. At this point as an adult, I needed some different kind of guidance. I was moving into another season of my life and required someone with more experience in life for what I was getting ready to walk into. God was right on time with his intentions to make sure that I was prepared for everything I was getting ready to deal with unknowingly. I got down there and dealt with all these different injuries my first year and at the time she was my assistant coach. But after getting through that first year she was no longer my assistant coach and we were close when she decided to step down but we were not as close as we are now.

Angel #2 is five years older than me and she is a mother. She just had her stuff together, at least that's what it seemed like on the outside. She was young but very mature in the way that she carried herself. Her maturity was definitely a lot further than her age and when it came to guidance this is who most of us when we wanted to have a reasonable conversation or some logic that we really didn't wanna hear but we knew we probably needed to hear, this is who we went to. From going into her office and not being able to curse because a cursing jar was in there, to watching her have her son in the gym or on the road late at night and being a single parent, she just carried herself in a manner that you wanted her as a mentor. I didn't set out intentionally for her to be my mentor. It literally happened that way based on the things that began to happen my second year down there. When she stepped down and decided to stop coaching I was recovering from my injury that summer. I ended up spending a lot of time at her house because I and my Teammates were having a spat. During the time I spent the summer with her, I started to go to church with her. During that time she was fasting and praying. She was the first person I ever saw on her face at home going complete in, just her and God. I remember staying the night at her house and I would hear her wake up at three-four o'clock in the morning, praying! She was praying for her future and praying for her son's future and praying for her future husband just speaking things as though they were. This was a new thing to me. As intriguing as it was it still wasn't intriguing enough for me to get up and do it lol. But it showed me a different level of "the walk" that I hadn't seen. I didn't understand when I would watch her go into praise and worship at church. I didn't understand when we would go visit churches, It seemed as though the Pastor's always had a word specifically for her. Most people go to church and the sermon is relatable, NO, God was sending specific messages to her and she was constantly being spoken over. I didn't understand it but I remember wondering like, "What do I have to do for me to get in good with God like that?" lol. It was at that moment, with that thought that God would start me on a journey not only to answer my question but also to show me how personal this thing is. He began to show me praise and worship as a combination of testimony and experience. How someone praises or worships is a reflection of what they have been through, so he taught me to never ask for another person's praise because you don't know what that person is going through or gone through for that praise to come out that way. I didn't know that while I was watching her go in at church, while I was hearing her go in at home in private, while I was watching God send specific directions and words for her; Its because of the things that she was struggling with behind closed doors. So the closer we got and the more I begin to learn about her opened my eyes to the reality of spiritual battles. This was all super new to me but the process of watching her wake up early in the morning pray, get ready for school and go to work later on the day, we might have a football game for her son later on seemed all so simple because like most mothers she had the super-woman persona. I didn't understand why she would call me in the living room, dim the lights and turn worship music on and show me how to go into worship. I didn't understand why when she would take me to work in the morning she would make me read devotionals and speak over my day until I started seeing her go through battles.

My understanding of these tools she gave me was they were going to be necessities because war is always on the rise. The Bible speaks of armor plate at all times, being prepared, just having the right tools when war comes is a big part of the strategy. What she was doing was sharpening her tools for war. So when I started seeing her go through breakups and go through struggling with school and being a single mom, not being able to work the hours she needed to work because school was taken over her life, That's when it started to make sense to me. I started to understand why she was doing the things that she was doing in that season of her life when she had the time to. Because this season was on the rise, the season where she wouldn't have time to wake up in the morning because she was waking up to study. The time when she had no strength but she knew she had to make it her son game. The times when she is finally comfortable enough to give her all to a person and they turn around and hurt her. I watched her go through these seasons after I watched her have a season of being on her face. Pain and war don't have a set time to come. So in always being prepared by taking that time to set a place for you and God will give you confidence when those wars arise. She laid a foundation that was firm so when the ground began to shake a little she knew she was on solid ground and just had to withstand the moments. She accomplished the goal of finishing school, her son thrives and is well rounded, she was able to get herself out of that situation and experience true love later on down the line with no bitterness in her heart and no baggage from that situation.

I was rebaptized. May 3, 2015, I went down in the water but this time I knew what I was going down for. I knew who God was, I knew my relationship with him, I knew how to get to him and I was beyond grateful for the people that he sent to get me back to his place that I had got so far away from. Or better yet I won't even say I got so far away from this place that I didn't know this place existed because I can't lie and say the things that I know now I knew growing up even in the church that I grew up in. With all the things that I was learning from Angel #2, I also saw the value in the gift that God had given her. She is a true prayer warrior. When you are young in your faith, you feel like those people are the people who pray to God the loudest. Those people who can pray and it feels like it's just natural to them and it carries anointing, and you on the other hand can't pray without being distracted in your mind or you just feel like you don't have the words to say because it doesn't sound like those people. Having that mentally has you leaning on those people a lot more than you should. When I was going through hard times or when something hit me right at that moment I would call her and ask her to pray for me. She would, and I know you're probably reading this like "well what's wrong with that ain't that what good friends do?", it is. In fact, that's what great friends do, but at what point did I stop and go to the throne myself? The same access she had to God I also had, so why wasn't my first instinct to go to him myself before requesting someone else to come on my behalf. See what I learned at this time was my prayers are supposed to be on the mainline lol. When I request help it just backs up, touching and agreeing. Well while God was showing me this error I started to ask him how I could correct it. He laid on my heart to fast. Now me being so immature in my faith I'm thinking he is talking about food or something. But he meant this person that I pretty much talked to every day.

Angel #2 had a trip coming up which she would be leaving the country. She would be gone for a decent amount of time and God was pretty much telling me that during her time of being away take that time to get on my face by myself. At the time of his revealing this strategy to me, I was dealing with a nose injury. Due to a break in my nose, my right nasal passage was being blocked. I also had very narrow sinus passages and a balloon of air that sat behind the bridge of my nose that caused extreme pressure in my face. These issues caused a lot of migraines, trouble with balance, sudden fainting, blurred vision, and vertigo. When I moved back to Michigan after graduation all of these symptoms got worse and at the time I didn't know about anything other than the broken nose. When I arrived home I was out of work and at the quickness of how bad my health was getting, I wouldn't be able to work. I had all kinds of issues getting insurance and then once I got it, it took forever for me to find a doctor. Spent days, in fact, months in my room in my bed. I slept whole days away because of these headaches. I barely ate because I was always nauseous. I was so confused at all of this happening so I didn't spend a lot of time with God. I prayed but it was so many other things I could've been doing during that time in process of heading to my healing.

So I got to work... I let my sister in Christ enjoy her vacation and even when we did talk I didn't mention my emotional state. I didn't mention anything about what I was going through, I begin to pray more. I begin to get in my bible more. I begin to read more devotionals that connected to how I was feeling. Some days I felt discouraged because I was doing all this and still was waking up in this horrible pain and cloudy state. See in most cases we want God to be a microwavable God. We want him to move when we want him to move and often we can get caught up in the idea of 'I'm doing what I'm supposed to be doing so why am I not healed?" The best advice I can give in this mind state is to understand that what is a day to us is but a minute to God. Also, understand that faith is a muscle. For a Muscle to become strong, it has to go under major amounts of pressure consistently. After working on a particular muscle area you start to see what we know as "Gains". This is exactly how our faith works. We can't develop faith if we are never in situations that test the current level of our faith. This was one of my levels and it was time for me to go to another one.

God then led me to read the book of Job in the bible. Overall the story is about a man with who God and the devil were having a conversation about. The man was a man of God and the devil pretty much wanted to prove to God that if he went through enough things he would turn away from God. But God knew Job, he knew his heart so he assured the devil that he would not turn from him. He allowed the Devil to do everything to Job except kill him. Job lost his whole family, wife, and kids included. Then Job was struck with disease and literally anything else you can think of. But even in his troubled state he never turned on God. Eventually, God gave Job everything he lost back and more 10 fold. Now I'm not comparing my situation to Job's but what I took from this story was the process of faith. Believing in the darkest times of what you know to be true, that God will always move on your behalf no matter what things may currently look like. Job didn't know if what he was going through would ever come to an end but he knew his life was much better with acknowledging God than not. Sometimes when we get caught up in what's happening to us it's hard for us to grab onto something, that's why that faith has to be so close and nearby it's our safe haven. It's our glue in this crazy life game of tag lol.

Now even after reading this amazing story I still was waking up in pain, still was trying to filter how much I talked to my sister and trying to figure out how and when this healing God was gonna do was gonna happen. My little brother had a doctor's appointment. My mom had to work so she asked my Grandfather Butch to take him. But my mom figured he would get lost so she asked me to ride with them. We got to the hospital downtown, he parked the car in valet the car and we went in. Of course, when we went in we found out it was the wrong place and needed to go to another building. We walked back out and waited for the car to come back up. While we were waiting it was a valet guy standing to my left that was just kind of looking at me. I honestly started to feel uncomfortable and had a migraine coming on so I was beyond ready to go at that moment. Then our car pulled up and as I started walking towards the car, my headache in full-blown motion now, the young man leaned over and touched my elbow. When he touched my elbow he said: "The spirit of the Lord told me to tell you to believe, He told me to tell you yes it's him you are hearing, stop second-guessing it." After he said that I stood there in aww, he then began to tell me his testimony, after we talked for a good 10-15 minutes. I got in the car and we headed to another hospital. What I didn't realize was after the young man touched my elbow my headache completely went away. See what I was on my face for was that moment, extremely unexpected but right on time. God knew mentally where I was. He knew I was trying to be positive but was getting tired in that fight. He knew my appointment would be scheduled not long after this encounter but I needed this to hold me until I got the news that he already knew. What I need us to understand is I am not saying doing what I'm suppose to do is What has to be done for the exchange of what God has in his hands. I don't want anyone to think I am saying if you do this, this and this then God will give you what I ask for. Again he is not genie. But understand the importance of all this is, the process. The process of me just seeking him on my own behalf. As I'm sure you know this encouraged me. I got more in my word, I prayed even more, I spoke healing strongly over myself in expectation of him to do just what his word said he would. This was the process that God intended for me to go through. See sometimes we can become so dependent on other people for our salvation we forget that it's OURS. We forget how to pray for ourselves. God literally knows everything we are going through, every emotion, every thought, in most cases he just wants to hear us say it out of our own mouths. This time when my spiritual crutch was kicked from under me I feel like I responded the way I was supposed to... I walked.

Isolation for elevation

Summer after my last semester of undergrad I went to Missouri for three months for my internship. At the time I was at the end and I needed an internship for graduation. We went to the national tournament for the second year that year and every year when your team gets there we have a community service project. The year before our community service project was a place called Drumm Farm Center for Children. The first year due to the rain most of the time we weren't really able to get off the bus to do anything. The following year I was so intrigued by the little bit that we did learn the year before, I ended up reaching out for an internship. We ended up coming to Drumm the second year and I connected with a Lady named Lisa. We had a small conversation and I remember asking, "I wanna know why its not more places like this in the United States", Her response was, "Nobody really knows about us so maybe now we just need the right people to get us out there so we can expand". I decided then that I needed to be there so when I got back to the house I did everything I needed to do to settle the paperwork. I told them I was interested. The situation ended up being I would get paid $200 every two weeks. I was paying for the internship out of my pocket so I would put $150 towards my school payments and keep $50 to get food or gas with. So the problem is if I'm spending the $200 on the internship I didn't really have money to live while I was there. I lived in a tiny house on the farm. I was on my own and I had to figure out how I was gonna live, at least that's what I thought.

The beautiful thing about God is when you belong to him he shows himself strong and evident in your life. I had just gone through being baptized and all of these great things months prior and now I'm in this place of solitude away from my best friends, away from my family, away from everything that makes me comfortable. I knew very well this was intentional. It is very easy for followers of Christ to get caught up in What God is doing for you when everything is going well. I was on full scholarship. I was passing school with flying colors. The church was great. Everything in my life seemed to be in this amazing place and I had to move to this place by myself and be broke. Not only was I broke by the time I got ready to move there I started having teeth problems. When I arrived in Missouri I had a really bad infection in one of my teeth and I couldn't eat solid food. I just adjusted to the situation and kept it moving.

When I got to the farm I made it intentional effort to spend more time with God. I used up my time either working out or reading books and my bible. I started trying to memorize Bible verses. The ones that I would memorize I would stick them up on my wall. I set alarms to get up for Prayer an hour earlier than I needed to be to set my day. I was intentional in seeking God in that particular time of my life. I knew from past experiences that it would take these things implemented in my life for me to grow and be able to move forward on my own. The goal is to not get stagnant or create idols out of the people that he was using to teach me. So I was intentional during the season and I definitely think he began to truly show himself through the things that begin to manifest while I was in solitude. Know that God uses people not only to teach us during our walk but also to use others to be a reflection of him in some of our hardest times. Those people exhibit compassion, support, and helping hands just at the right time. When I first got to Missouri my car broke down probably like a week later. I remember coming into work one morning and I was telling the woman I was interning under what was going on with my car. She offered for her husband to take my car to his mechanic to be looked at. After the car was looked at I found out what was going on and it was gonna be pretty expensive. Of course, my family was helping pay my tuition so paying for my car to get fixed just wasn't in the budget. After I received the call about the car I hung up and called my family. Once I realized it was out of my hands I remember going to bed and just feeling discouraged. But the next morning I woke up and I went outside because Lisa, whom I was interning under, text me and told me that my car had been towed back to the house or brought back to the house. I went outside and a receipt for my car being fixed was in the cupholder.

This situation gave me a boost of confidence and assured me that God was with me. I went to work every morning with a toothache, no complaints. I just went to work. One day I remember Lisa taking me out to eat for lunch. She noticed all I was eating was soft food. At the time I wasn't telling anybody what I was going through with my teeth other than my family. I didn't tell because I was there to work and I would deal with my teeth whenever I could. She asked me what was going on and I told her that one of my teeth broke and got infected and I was just trying to keep food out of it so this is my way of doing it. A couple of days later she told me she had reached out to one of the donors who happened to be a Dentist. Her husband was actually a dentist as well and she told him about my situation. The Lady brought me in to get x-rays done and she sat me down. She told me everything that was going on my teeth and pretty much at 25 years old I was at the risk of losing my back teeth because I had gone this long without going to the Dentist. I sat there with tears in my eyes because unfortunately this situation was just kind of out of my control. I didn't have insurance. I couldn't afford insurance at the time. She looked at me and said,

`` I'm sending you out to my husband. He will do all the hard work. Once he's done he'll send you back to me for deep cleaning. All I ask is that you pay it forward to someone in the future".

I got over $45,000 worth of dental work done on my mouth for absolutely free. I walked into the Dentist, They checked my name in and I would go ahead and come out with no problems. Some days I would be there for long periods of time and Some days it was quick in and out. This was my first full-blown experience of God moving urgently to deal with any of my needs. There were no delays in this particular season of my life. By the time the need would arise the solution would follow right after. Sure enough, he looked out with the internship and me being able to pay for it in even with the fixing of my car but my teeth too Lord? Aww, this was something different, this was the I care about them big and small things, God! Still to this day blows my mind about just how that worked out because I was in so much pain. Although I felt like it was a small thing compared to the things God put in front of me and the dreams that were important to me, he didn't think it was.

I am literally going to say about a week after I started getting the majority of the work done I was having another conversation with my boss and I'm not sure how the idea of the newspaper came about but she told me that someone from the Independence Newspaper wanted to come to talk to me about my story. The story of my process of getting recruited and how I ended up in Tennessee, how I ended up in Independence, and my goals of having my own nonprofit Someday. A young girl came in and I remember specifically wearing my Detroit Tigers T-shirt that day just to be a representation of my city. We talked and I gave her the story. About a week or so later I was on the front page of the paper. I remember everybody being so excited about the article it was literally probably one of the proudest moments of my life for multiple reasons. I was proud because I was able to be a positive light for my city. Here I am the city girl who has gone off and kind of reinvented herself. I live on a farm in a small house, it's a very different journey. I was also able to show my appreciation to a lot of people I felt were responsible for molding me into who I am.

Not long after the interview, we were getting ready for this big dinner Drumm had every year. At the time during the day, I was ripping
and running, picking up flowers and everything to try to get ready for
the day. I got a call from the front office telling me to come to the office
when I got back to the farm. When I got into the office I walked in to
see a man I had never met in my life. He handed me an envelope and
told me that he saw my story in the paper and he loved it and it was
truly inspirational and he just wanted to donate my life. He then hands
me a $500 check. But that's not the exciting part it is but it's not, the
exciting part is I had $500 left to pay on my tuition for school. I wasn't
having to wait years to see that God could provide for me. I didn't have
to wait years to see that God wanted to heal my body. I was literally experiencing him tend to my every need during a time where I was completely out of my comfort zone.

It was also during this time that I saw the way the church is supposed to function in a believer's life. One of the biggest issues that this
generation specifically has with religion really stems from churches.
The Church has become such a circus and a visible place for hypocrisy.
When children encounter adults that don't sit well with their spirit
usually makes a child uncomfortable and they don't wanna be around a
person or they cry and run from the person. Think about the youth or
people who didn't grow up in church spiritually. They are children so
when they come into a church and they encounter all of these negative
experiences with these people who say they are the men and women
of God it makes them run away. It's the same reaction. Their maturity in their spiritual life is not strong enough for them to look past the
foolishness of these people just being human and getting to the source.
So the pedestal that church is put on and then what people experience
once they get in those churches don't match up a lot of times and that's
what our generation has an issue with. Although I truly understand this
and I know it is a big factor as to why I stayed away from church for so

long. If I could give any encouragement to my generation and the people younger than me, it would be:

Understand your relationship with God is personal. It's not dependent on anybody else, it's not dependent on a building, it's not dependent on religious statues. God desires a personal relationship. The structure of what church should be is to help you establish your foundation to build your communication with God. That's not the case at times but as you get older your value of things changed based on your experience with it. Seek Him personally and learn to accept proper correction. If you are on the other side of this be the proper correction. Correct with Grace just like God does us.

A lot of the things I learned about history or just life, in general, I learned from reading books on my own outside of the classroom. The things that the teacher says to you but don't necessarily pertain to the lesson plan or even to school are the things that stick with you throughout life. You may have that student never receive or understand something you teach them but if you are ever put in position where you have to discipline them, How you discipline them matters. Correct discipline makes them respect you. They will always remember the lesson that you taught them in that moment. This is the same thing with our faith. Understanding the student shows the teacher desires to guide the student and give you all of the lessons that you need to maneuver through this life but it's just figuring out the best way to get to your student so that they view discipline as correction and not as something negative or judgmental. Because God is always there with us, trying to figure out our connection and how we hear him and how we communicate with him, or how he talks to us those are the lessons in the maturity of growing you in your faith. Then the same people who are supposed to be God's people and help the needy and help the poor we know situations happen a lot of things are exposed. Then churches seem just as Shiesty sometimes as a regular people off the street. Although humans are humans whether in the church or outside the church the reality is people in the world have put the people of the church on a pedestal. And just like a leader of a corporation Has to know their title means that they have to carry a certain image regardless of them being a human who makes mistakes they still have to carry themselves a certain way. The best example I can give here is athletes who know that their image is their brand if they do something crazy they can kill their brand or they can lose their Endorsements and sometimes lose their job. This is the same thing with God's people when we don't move in a manner based on the anointing that we say is on our life or is told is on our lives than the people who are supposed to see our light don't see it that way and it messes up or distorts the light that was suppose to be reflected to people. It messes up your credibility and then it makes it hard for people to look at you as that man or woman of God that you may be but do not carry yourself in that manner. We have to understand that we are the holders of light, we are to be a reflection of who God is so when we don't move in that manner then it's hard for non-believers to even consider becoming believers.

My whole point of going down that rabbit hole is at this time the church that I had joined was extremely small and it was a storefront church. Now our member size wasn't large at all but these people had the heart and spirit of God within that small place. When I was away and away from my family and even away from them they made sure that I got canned goods. They made sure that they took in an offering for me every week for church and they would send me something just to have money in my pocket. I can tell you as a child of God who was new in this part of the walk of my faith it definitely encouraged me to understand that God's people do exist. The church can have such a bad reputation as I said because of people not reflecting just the kindness and generosity and love of God. Being a woman or a man of God does not mean that you walk in perfection, it means that you walk in acknowledgment of who you belong to and where your strength comes from. You understand you are a servant. The moment you understand everything you come in contact with to accomplish anything is due to the grace of God then it opens your heart up for humility for God's people. Because the reality is if you think you are doing anything out of your own strength or out of the fact that you are just a good person that is how egos grow because you're not doing it out of the sense of I knew that this is God's doing. He's going to get the glory out of it at the day. If you are looking for your own glory then your perception ruins the potential blessing and connection with God's people.

While I always felt like going to church was enough and when all those other areas of my life began to grow I thought I was doing enough. But what I can tell people from experience is that serving is a big part of your relationship with God. It's cool to do nice things for people you love but can you do it with people you don't know? Can you do it with people who are more spiritually mature than you? Submission comes in all different shapes and sizes and that's how I looked at serving God's people. While I was learning the spiritual side of serving I do believe that the season of my life of being a youth leader was preparing me for what was to come. I was knee-deep in youth when God began to speak to me about going home. But I had been so lit with what God had done for me the summer of being in Missouri and during my time back in Tennessee I just knew he was gonna help me start my own mentoring program because I had a business plan. I had the contacts I just needed to pull it together. I went home with expectations of God making me a business owner and me kicking my public speaking career off while starting Grad school. My God was I BIG Wrong!

I got home and God made me a teacher lol. I'm talking about threw me directly into the fire. I started as a Paraprofessional and eventually would become a long-term substitute for 7th and 8th graders. I knew God had called me to speak to the youth and to be a mentor but I definitely did not think this is what he meant by that. Them 7th and 8th graders made a woman out of me though. The same preparation I went through when preparing for youth Sunday I had to implement that into teaching. I knew when I came to class that if I wasn't prepared ahead of time then it was gonna be a long day. I tapped into the things I remember seeing my teachers from middle school do. Staying over an hour or so after school just to get prepped for the next day. I started to understand the kids on a different level. The more days passed I started to see he had been preparing me for this moment for years. He had been grooming me into a leader, he had been clearing me of my stage fright, he had developed the very areas most people go to school for. I remember when I started posting the things I was doing with the kids on social media and the discussions I would have, the teachers who I held at the highest point of educators started saying "You got IT". They started giving me compliments and it confirmed what I had always heard. When God leads you to something, know that even if you don't understand it, it's a purpose for it. One season is always preparation for something in the next or the next. God is never gonna give you tools or gifts that he doesn't intend to sharpen for use. I had a word spoken over my life. The word was, "God said he is going to use you like his voice, you are going to speak for him". I knew I loved speaking, so I just knew being a motivational speaker of some sort was my calling. But when the teaching thing came about I started to realize that this is why we must stick out the course of what God's plan is so that we can get understanding and actually walk properly into what we should. Because we can take those words and make them out to be something that wasn't even a part of the plan. When God sends word through another vessel in the prophetic, direction will follow. It may not follow right away but it follows.

Lessons Learned

As I am in this current season of my life I can look back over the last 5-6 years of my life with a lot more clarity and understanding. I literally found myself at a time in my life where I felt like I had all these puzzle pieces in my hands and when I would finally start putting them together and getting a picture, it was always one or two that I couldn't figure out where they went. Rather it was the injuries I had to endure in college or me going to school for Business and ending up in Education. These are just a few of the many pieces I was having a hard time figuring out what was the reason for these pieces and how they would be useful to my picture. But now I get it and I owe that to the processing of my relationship with God.

My relationship with Him didn't grow until I left the church. Now I am not saying this is the route for everyone to go, what I am saying is the building and even the people sometimes can be a bigger distraction from what you are truly there for... The relationship. But even still God will get to you. It was two people through experience for me. Know that you are the church, you are the building, you are a place where God dwells, you are the container of the light. So just like the church's image is to be the light and draw people, we as people have the same responsibility. We literally have the same ability to draw people to want to get saved, they don't have to wait on an altar call at church. But that all starts with us realizing our relationship is personal because all of us are different. Our stories are different, our paths are different and most importantly our purpose is different.

See if I didn't know God for myself it's so many different things that I would have missed, so many lessons I wouldn't have learned, and still, so much confusion would dwell within my life. My path is a little calmer now because I know how to use the tools that I and God came up with within the midst of my storms. Because of my relationship, I know my personal strategy and that understanding holds more value than my church attendance. But my view of the church has also changed. In building that personal relationship I realized that the church is just another source, a place for fellowship, an added resource to what I and God have already developed. It's like living with a teacher as a parent and then going to school for extra teaching. That parent is gonna instill things in you that will help and it will come in a more relatable manner from that parent because of your relationship. But then you go to school to learn those different teachings in more depth and from different people, with different perceptions and experiences. That's the hearing of testimonies, seeing the pain and emotion of a person in praise in worship. That's hearing the word from a man or woman of God who can give you a different perception of something that God may have already shown you. So now I no longer put this huge expectation on the church to be this perfect building where God is because I know the God I serve doesn't even dwell in perfect people. After all, he dwells in me.

5

Pain Can Change

They didn't tell us:

There are different levels of grief

This is one of the most vulnerable states for your spirit to be attacked.

Grief can kill you

Dealing with death is a process with many layers to it.

Life doesn't stop because death comes.

Death is one of those things where if you don't take the time to actually figure out what's going on with you, it could overtake your life. Dealing with grief at a very early age, I think I thought I had become numb to it. It wasn't until I felt the pain of losing people who were part of my everyday life that I truly understood the depths Of how deep grief can go and how it can affect so many different things in your life. This will probably be one of my hardest chapters to write, but I will be brutally honest and completely transparent. I'm going to be this way because I feel like this chapter will be super important to many people. I'm taking you through every emotion, every part of my healing that I had to go through for me to get to the place where I am now. I think because many people see me now and think everything is good, but I'm dealing, and I'm coping with the loss of my sister a lot better now than I have in the past. I take no credit for it because God legit had to intervene to save me from myself. But in that saving, he also taught me a lot of things in the process as well.

No matter what, death is part of life. We can't get away from it. But death, especially when close to you, can be very harsh to handle mentally, physically, and emotionally. Without the right people in your corner, you can easily end up in the same place as the person you are grieving for. During my experience with grief, I experienced my first bout with depression and saw how people develop habits while going through that process. Through the almost 2 years up until this point of her being gone, no one except my close friends truly know what I went through after losing my sister. I lost two very important people to me in back-to-back years, and I can truthfully say it affected me a lot more than I was willing to admit at the time.

My sister and I are 2 years and 2 weeks apart. I met 3 of my siblings at the age of 8: my oldest sister Nette, sister Tyne, and little brother Tank. Most people, when they see us say that, Myself, Tyne and Tank look just alike. We instantly clicked once we were introduced. Over the years, our relationships would change, but I think honestly, it was part of our growing up. Tyne and I really started to have these big sister little sister moments. We would have these falling outs that lasted for weeks where we wouldn't talk. Even still, until today, I laugh about how I genuinely never understood what half our beef was about, lol. The crazy part would be whether we were talking or not. I take pride in being a sister, especially when she needed me the most. No matter if it was her or my niece in need, if she called, I came running. If she needed a break, I took my niece for days. I watched her work herself to the point where she would cause her body to go into a Lupus flare due to the amount of stress she put on herself.

My sister and I had gotten into some kind of dispute, which led to us not talking for months. I believe it was something that her boyfriend at the time had posted, and she didn't like the way I responded. So this led to her deleting me from social media altogether. To this day, I still think it's the funniest thing in the world because I remember thinking, "this girl is really crazy." The dude and I disagreed, agreed to disagree, then kept it moving. We were fine. Man, she wasn't having it, lol, so boom, I'm deleted from social media. My dad would often ask me if I had talked to Tyne, and I would say, "no, your child is not talking to me," lol. So finally he asked me why and I told him. I also told him I would not be fixing this situation. Anyone who knows me knows I do not do conflict. So I am usually the first to apologize even if I'm not wrong, but not this time, and I stood on that. I felt really powerful. Like, "yeah, I'm taking a stand"! Lol. The whole time I was acting just as petty and stubborn as her. This literally led to us not talking from March to Thanksgiving.

Thanksgiving was at my Dad's that year, and we were all in the basement. Even then, we really didn't say much to each other. I believe we talked about my niece's face because she had a black eye from jumping off the couch and hitting her nose on a table. Other than that, we didn't say much to each other. After Thanksgiving, it went back to the same thing, but what hurt me most was that I also wasn't speaking to or seeing my niece that often. Anyone who knew me during that time of my life knew I always had my niece, but I didn't during the majority of this time of going without talking to her.

Fast forward to Christmas Eve, I walked into my cousin's house. Usually, I'm the late one, but I was the first one out of my siblings there this time. As I sat around after greeting the rest of my family, I couldn't help but feel this weird feeling. So I asked my dad where everybody was, and he told me my oldest sister was on the way and that he hadn't talked to my brother. He then informed me that my sister Tyne was in the hospital. Now at this point, I was pissed because she had been in there for a couple of days, and no one had told me anything. I proceeded to ask what was going on, and they informed me that she had a lupus flare. We had not talked like I said since Thanksgiving, but the next morning, Christmas Day, the first thing I did was head to that hospital. No matter what was going on between us, I never wanted her to feel like she was battling anything alone. I know she had a lot of support, but this was my big sister, my TyTy mommy. I wanted to be there even the times she didn't call me herself. I went to the hospital that day and once more before the year was out. She asked me to come in and twist her hair, so I did. I twisted her hair and oiled her scalp. We talked about our Dad and brother and her plans for Tylar. We talked about the things that she desired for herself. She wanted to do a lifestyle change, so we sat and thought of a workout plan, and she wanted to go on a diet, so we started trying to figure that out. It was just a good conversation, and then after a while, we just kind of sat in the room in silence. It never occurred to me at that moment that would be the last time that I would see my sister alive. I left there, and I went to a football game. One of my college teammates' brothers played for Georgia Tech and his parents got me a ticket to come to the game they were playing at Ford Field, so I went to show my support. I went to the hospital and hung out with my sister, then went to the game.

My sister came home on New Year's Day or the day after; I can't remember which one. Her birthday is January 3rd. She was home, and the plan was she wanted to spend her birthday with my niece. She hadn't been able to be around for Christmas, so she just wanted to be with her baby. She went out to dinner for her birthday, and I believe the plan was we were supposed to go to this game place or something that Sunday to celebrate her birthday all together. She wanted to do something fun that my niece could be involved with. So at the time, my Father and I were working together, and I remember coming into his classroom earlier that week on probably like the fourth, and my dad was telling me that he thinks she's going to have to go back to the hospital. Her body had begun to bruise, so we knew that was the sign of another flare. But knowing what she was going through, I just wanted to give her time and space to enjoy being around my niece, her boyfriend, and her family. We texted throughout the week, but I didn't go to see her. I just checked on her, and we would have small talk. We talked about her birthday, and then we talked about mine. So on that Saturday, she sent me a text saying that she was back in the hospital. I'm like, "aww man, what's wrong?" and she texted me back and said, "it's my heart, I'm in ICU" and I'm like, "OK, where are you, back at Harper?" she replied, "Yes. ' So I said, "OK, I'm going to come down, and I'm going to stay with you, and I'll just go to church from there." Now at the time, I was sharing cars with my Mother, and we were all sitting at the table at my Grandmother's house when I got the text. I told my mom "hey Ima take you home, and I'm going to spend the night at the hospital with Tynecia tonight, and I'll be back in the morning to get ready for church" and she said "Ok."

By the time I got to the car, my sister had texted me back and told me not to come there. She said it was late and that they would not allow me to stay or come into the ICU at that time of night. Looking back is always interesting to me on this particular day because if anybody knows anything about my sister she never denies anybody coming to the hospital. She always wants somebody there. So for her to tell me not to come at the time, I wasn't looking at it like it was a weird thing. I just was like, I didn't know anything, so I'm like, "OK, alright, well, I'll be there tomorrow as soon as I get out of the church." I said I love you, and she said, I love you too, and that's the last conversation I had with my sister. I got up the next morning doing my normal routine for church. I got up about an hour and a half before it was time for me to go to church. I got dressed, and I'm listening to praise and worship music getting myself together. I got in the car, and I got to the corner of my street, and my phone rings, and it's my baby brother Tank, and he is crying. He's crying, and the only thing he could say was, "Shan! Shan! Shan! She's gone!" I'm like, "what are you talking about Tank, who is gone?" and he said, "she gone Shan, Tyne is gone. She passed away". "Tank you lying I just talked to her!" I kept repeating it until finally, I just started screaming. I couldn't comprehend that my sister was gone. My sister was 28 years old; she was too young. I feel like she had a whole life to live so at that moment, I couldn't comprehend it. I was paralyzed at the time, like I couldn't move. I'm in the driver's seat sitting at the end of the block, and I'm crying, and I just couldn't press and go to church. I drove across State fair to the other side of my street, and I pulled over, and I just cried. I grabbed my phone, and I called my Mother, who was doing hair in the house. But when I called, I couldn't get it out, I said "Ma!" And I just started crying and screaming, and my mom told me she thought I had gotten into a car accident. She screamed, asking me what was wrong, and I'm like, "ma, she gone, she gone, my sister is gone!". When I finally got the strength, I turned around and went back home. My mom met me at the door. I will never forget this moment because I tell people I don't come from an affectionate family, But when I got to the house, my mom was already standing on the porch, and I just fell into her arms and I just cried and she held me tighter than she ever held me before.

Your will be done

Before my sister's passing, when she would ask me to pray for her or go into the hospital, I would always pray for Healing. God, please "Heal her from the crown of her head to the soles of her feet". God, you healed such and such in the Bible. God, your word says that you were Healer, that you are a way maker. God, you make everything whole. So that is my expectation for this situation. I expect you to do what you told me you do". I was going to make God stand on what he said. This is the man that makes the sun come up; he assures the feeding of the birds. So it's nothing for him to heal my sister, right? Because this is what you told me you do, you in the healing business Jesus, this is what you do.

That was literally how I approached this situation every time. Sure enough, God would pull her through every time. So my faith was strong in that because I had seen him step in so many times. I had seen him pull her through every situation every single time. But this particular time, I'm not sure why but when my Dad told me that she would have to go back into the hospital, I remember saying something to God that I have never said in my life, especially not in this situation. Not understanding the magnitude of how serious things were, I said,

God, I know you are in the midst of the situation. And I trust you, and I ask that you cover her Lord, keep her protected, LET YOUR WILL BE DONE".

The "Your will be done " Prayer is one of the hardest prayers, scariest prayers to pray ever in life to me. Because in this situation, this is when you don't have anything left, so I have to depend on Him. I know the situation is completely out of my hands. This is a true testament to the fact that you literally don't know what else to do in a situation. You don't know what else your hands can control, so you have to say God whatever your will is that's what I want to be done, that's the ultimate trust in God and God revealed it to me because he asked me a question when everything was said and done. She was gone, and He asked me, "How do you feel about me when my will is not what you want or what you expect?" That was a question that I didn't know I would spend the next six months of my life trying to understand and answer. So at that moment, when I got to the hospital, and I saw my sister lying in this bed, no life but the most crispy eyebrows on the Eastside.. That's what I had in the back of my mind. But I'm upset with God because you were supposed to heal her! She got a daughter, she has a child she needs to be here for. How could you do this? You were supposed to heal her; I was expecting you to heal her! But even at that moment, I couldn't communicate the anger; I couldn't get it out because who am I to be mad at God? Who am I to be mad at the person who is in control of all. At least that's what I thought, and that's when God showed me that I wasn't coming to him in raw form. He needed me to figure out how to give him everything and not pick and choose what to hand over to him. He needed me to understand that he cared about EVERYTHING in my life, even when he did something that didn't seem fair to me.

See God doesn't just want us to come to him in prayer or just come to him in general when seeking guidance in situations. He wants us to come with the truth, nothing but the truth, so help me God. No matter how hard the truth is, he knows it already. He is just waiting on you to say it. It's like confessing sorry when you are in a bad relationship. The best thing to do is to communicate when you have an issue because now the issue is out on the table, and both parties can come together and figure out how they feel about this issue. Ima put my feelings on the table, and you put your Feelings on the table then we can decide from that point on what we're gonna do so we can move on with a plan of action. The point of this is so that we don't run from another situation like this that we may run into again down the line. This process will make our relationship stronger, and that is exactly what God wants. He wants you in raw form because once you get through this situation with him and tell him exactly how you feel and what's going on with you, he can move you to the next season. Now y'all relationship will grow in that moment to get you over whatever hump is producing the frustration even if its with him. But if you're not coming to him that way, your relationship will continue to run into that same problem until it's addressed or until the relationship dissolves altogether because you're not truly who you are supposed to be with this person. If you can not truly tell someone you love and who claims they love you how you really feel, then you don't love them enough. God knew I was mad at him. So again, the question is, "Will you trust me even when my will isn't what you want?". So now, not only has God exposed that My faith wasn't where I thought it was, but I also couldn't communicate that to him, so now I got a communication issue that I didn't even know I had until this point.

I didn't know until this revelation during this whole grieving process that I didn't deal with conflict well. As I stated earlier, I was mad, but I couldn't say that to God. He showed me months later that I had an issue with communicating my feelings without fear of losing someone. I had grown up my whole life and never saw healthy conflict, which made me conceal my feelings and just take things on the chin versus confronting situations and being able to express my feelings healthily. When you grow up in a household where every argument or disagreement results in fighting or full-blown grudges being held, you grow up to think that that is what expressing your feelings gets you. So instead of me being able to express when something was bothering me or when I was upset about something, I would just keep it to myself to avoid a conflict with the person out of fear of our relationship being ruined. Not understanding that I was even bringing that into my relationship with God, but this moment is when I started understanding grace a lot more because no matter what you do or how you feel, God's Grace extends. It's there, and once I begin to understand what I was dealing with internally, my view of my sister's transition begins to change.

This is why I love God because he doesn't wait once something is out on the table. He moves right at that moment to start fixing the situation and bringing forth deliverance. So at the moment where I'm realizing that I'm upset with God, he put me in a situation that I reflected on for two weeks after it happened, and this is how all these other things were revealed to me.

When I got to the hospital after seeing my sister and acknowledging my family when it was time to go, my Father asked me to do something that I was not expecting. First, my sister's Mother pulled my older sister and me to the side and asked us or told us that we were the ones that we're gonna have to handle this funeral, so this is the first blow I got hit with. She tells us that we have to do the funeral because she can't, so at that moment, I had to step into the older sibling role that I've never had to step into. I've never had to plan a funeral a day in my life. I've been to a lot of them, but I've never had to plan a funeral. So now I'm helping plan my first funeral and the funeral of someone I shared a face with. So that's that situation, but then my Dad came up to me, and my Dad asked me to pray before we all had to leave the hospital. So I'm thinking he wanted us to pray in the lobby area where we all were, But no, he wanted us to pray over my sister before we left. So I went back into the room, and I'm next to her bed, and everyone came around, and we made this big circle inside the room that went out into the hallway. Now before I get into the prayer, I need you to understand what is happening to me at this moment. Up until this time, I had the worst anxiety about praying out loud in front of people. So when my Dad asked me to do this, I was like, oh my God, like I'm already a wreck; why are you asking me to do this. But I'm not gonna tell my Dad No, especially not in a situation like this. So I go in the room and we pray. At this moment, this is again why I said I love God because the two things that I just explained to you that eventually were revealed to me about myself over the months to come started in this moment. Not only did I have to address what I was angry with him about, but I also had to address it right there at that moment. I had to feel those feelings right there in front of everybody. Now, if you've never experienced an extreme amount of guilt and grief, I can tell you that those emotions are completely uncontrollable, so at that moment, God got exactly how I felt.

Lord, we come to you as humble as we can with tears in our eyes and pain in our hearts. Lord, this HURTS, and we don't understand it, but I know if it's your will, it's not meant for us to understand. We accept your decision, Lord. We trust that you were here and that Tyne was at peace and held no fear as she prepared to see you. We thank you for the time that we were able to have with her lord. We thank you for the gift that she left in Tylar. We ask that you continue to cover our family and her child as we move forward and try to find comfort in your decision. Amen

Addiction

So now I'm in this place where God has asked me this question, and I don't know how to answer, so now that journey begins. The prayer kind of kicked the whole situation off for me and I would go on just learning more about myself. I started to see myself in a different light, but I couldn't understand why he had exposed this to me. Now the thing about when God shows you something about yourself, that's not the end of it. He shows it, but now the work begins to deliver you from it. That's a hard process, But I'm more conscious of it now, so I'm able to push myself to continue to express my feelings and express frustration, and it's encouraged me in my prayer life. This was a needed foundation for God to establish in me at the beginning of this process with grief because he knew what was coming next. My sister passed on a Sunday that Monday, I think we were in the bar. I found myself in the bar like 3-4 days out of the week, and I can guarantee you I was meeting my father, my brother, and my sister there as well. A lot of us can testify that we started indulging in alcohol a lot during this time. Now personally, I'm not much of a drinker. I don't have too many vices or much of a vice at all. I occasionally drink but it's not something that I do daily. But

I was finding myself drinking almost every single day. Now for most people, I think they usually are like, "she's just going through something, so this is what she's doing" or whatever, just to kind of deal with the moment. But we don't understand how that turns into addiction very quickly, and literally, in the midst of me going through the grief, I realized I'm at the bar, I'm getting drunk. Like I'm not just drinking like I'm getting DRUNK, and I'm going home. I remember driving home, and I started talking out loud in the car like, "This ain't me." "You don't even drink like this; what are you doing?". The whole time, that's the spiritual side of me that I'm so grateful for. That was that Holy spirit because even when you don't have the strength to change something about yourself or deal with something like that, the Holy Spirit is always there. It shows itself in situations we really need it because I was literally falling into it this cycle, and I wasn't even paying attention.

We go through a traumatic experiences, and we as humans sometimes don't know how to deal with those emotions. I tell people all the time that I've lost a lot of people in my life. I thought I was becoming numb to death with the number of people that I was losing. But when my sister passed, and I had just lost my grandfather Butch the year before, that was a lot to take. Those are emotions and a type of pain that does not have words; no human words are created for that type of agony. I'm sure people who lose a parent or a child can understand Exactly what I'm saying. It's a certain type of trauma that cripples and snatches your emotions, and you don't know which way to go or how to deal with those emotions. They are super overwhelming, and that's what I was experiencing, and all along come to find out I was walking into a full-blown depression as well. Those moments where you find yourself wanting to sleep all the time and you don't want to talk. Then you start distancing yourself from everybody close and crying all the time. You just can't get out of this funk, grief snatches you into this dark place like that, and you don't even realize it. You tell yourself you are just gonna get through the day and look up, and months have passed. This is when having that strong village is a necessity. Because it's hard to be spiritually strong when you are in this place, you need people who know you and know to be in prayer for you even when you don't have the words to explain what's wrong. My friends were praying. They were there for me exactly when I needed them to be. Some missed a beat, but those who knew me and knew I wasn't myself were there. I can't say how much I appreciate that because they were a reflection of me. The alcohol or whatever the chosen vice hides you. It hides you from the world but inside, it exposes you to you very loudly.

Lesson Learned

What I learned through my grieving process was that I was human. I knew I was strong, but my strength wasn't enough for the battle of grief and depression. I also learned that all of those things are ok. Losing my sister showed me my mortality not so much in the idea of death but the idea of life. In this life, Marvin Gaye said it best, "It's only three things that's for sure, Taxes, Death and Trouble." I'm not exempt from pain, no matter how good of a person I thought I was. But I also wasn't exempt from his correction in the midst of that pain. The same way life doesn't stop just because something happens to us is the same way God functions. The pain we feel doesn't deter his plans. As unfair as I thought he was exposing me to me in the middle of my grief, I understood why he had to do it then. Sometimes the pain is the only thing that can slow us down enough for us to go through change. Pain is the time when God knows he has our undivided attention because it's a place of confusion and usually the time when we seek him most.

So boom, I'm an alcoholic now, LOL. But I've bought myself an OK excuse, "I know this hurts but you got to stop drinking", so I stopped drinking. I didn't drink for about two or three months after I had that moment. But then I found myself looking to replace that mini addiction I was developing. I started looking for affection because just like with alcohol, I needed something to make me feel something other than numbness. My sister died in the winter in January. That summer, I'd lose my virginity. The person I lost it to I had a lot of love for. I might even at some point say I was in love with this person, but when I tell you God was screaming no to me from the beginning of the situation, I don't say that lightly. The way that situation played out, he showed me just how out of character I had gotten. I've always said I would never be that girl. I never wanted to be the cause of another woman's pain and here I was willingly and knowingly doing so just out of the sense of my own comfort. To say I had developed a full-blown soul tie to this man would be an understatement. But again, I started noticing a pattern about myself when I was feeling really sad and that numb feeling would come; that's when I desired him the most. Just like alcohol, he made me feel something.. rather it was lust or love, it didn't matter; I could feel something, and that's what I wanted. So when the numbness begins to be too much for me, I would find myself flirting a little more, texting a Lil more, requesting to see him more. We went through this cycle for a nice little while until, eventually, he was no longer in a relationship. Rather I was the cause of the end of that relationship or not, I'm not sure, but it bothered me for a while. At this point in the situation God started showing me that I hadn't done anything except trade in one potential addiction for another one. I was still tryna fill a space in myself that only He could.

They didn't tell us that if you don't manage your emotions properly, they run wild. You find yourself doing things off impulse and not thinking about the long-term effects. I found myself dealing with my first pregnancy scare and some other health issues just out of my recklessness and lack of being able to control my emotions. Not only can unchecked emotions result in things like addiction, but they are also a manifestation of you jumping into situationships too quickly and wanting to engage in sexual activity when your emotional stability takes a dip. This is how toxicity between people becomes a part of their personality. Not only is it now a developed personality flaw, but it's how I dealt with emotions. I now live by this saying " Deal with you before anybody else has to." You and God are the only ones who have to deal with that toxic stuff with Grace because 9/10, the issue is only something you and Him can address. When other people are forced to deal with your unmanaged emotions, that's when we get these toxic relationships and friendships. This is when you get those children with people you know you had no business having a kid with, but you couldn't control your emotions and sent that I miss you text or that one for the road sex that still left lingering feelings, so you never made it to the road lol. Now you got a crazy baby mama/baby daddy that you stuck with. Most of us are born out of that toxicity, so we don't realize until it's too late at times that we are just repeating a cycle. I'm not saying everybody's reasons are the same, but I can assure you that the reason you can't leave that person alone is equal to that of a person with any other addiction, they either make you feel something, or they take away all feeling. Save yourself and others a lot of hurt by doing a self-check now and then. Know when you need to take time to heal and build yourself back up. Don't let your fear of looking weak or not wanting anyone to know you struggle to keep you in a cycle of filling voids with temporary things. I didn't know death would reveal these things to me, but I'm glad it did because I came out of that season of my life with a better prayer life and a more personal relationship with God. ?

6

Seasons

They didn't tell us that

Different seasons require different actions.

Knowing what season you are in is super important to know what actions to take.

New levels come with new devils

These cycles don't stop, just the things that affect us change when the seasons come back around.

Plans (Planting)

Figuring out positive ways to plant your feet is what should happen in this season. Start that business you've been wanting to start, go back to school, pick up a trade, learn something new that you didn't know. This is the Self-improvement stage. At this time prayer and meditation is very important. Talking to God about your goals is key but listening is just as important.

In this season Prayers need to be very specific. This is the time to strategize a plan, not with the expectation of these exact things playing out how you want but to give yourself some kind of path to follow. We get so caught up in these everyday life issues and everyday things that life throws that it is easy to get distracted. So this plan is a way for you to always have something to revert to. This is the time when you ask for strategy but ask for specific answers. Bare yourself at this moment.

Work Sheet

The plan

What exactly do you need from God?

What fruits of the spirit are gonna be necessary for you to focus on during this season?

What are the weaknesses that could keep you from accomplishing the goal?

One scripture to hold on to.

List Three specific questions for God in this current season of your life **(Pray over these questions and ask for wisdom and understanding whenever you are on your face)**

1.)

2.)

3.)

Figure it out (The Work)

When you can't see the fruits of your labor, and life is throwing things at you. You can and will fall, but you can't stay there. I've always found the saying "Failure isn't an option" quite funny. Because the reality is Failure may not be an option but it's a key ingredient in the recipe for success. I guarantee you there is no successful person in the world who has not gone through some type of failure. A lot of people may not talk about their failures but they happen. How do you learn something if you get it right all the time? I used to always tell my students the difference between certain cheaters is that some people cheat to learn new material and some people cheat just to get a good grade. The reason why I respect the cheater who cheated to learn more is that they are trying to put themselves in a position to never have to ask you for help again. If you do an assignment in class and you don't know what you're doing you're not able to cheat off anybody and you just wing it and you fail, you learned absolutely nothing and you didn't get a passing grade. One, you didn't allow yourself to see what you did wrong. Two, you didn't learn anything while you were cheating so now you don't even know why you got something wrong. The point of this season is to get moving. You can see your failure happen or success but what does it mean if you didn't actually go through the process. Learn something while you are working. Learn about yourself, Learn your passions. Results always require action. The two go hand in hand. In most cases, the place where the hindrance comes is after a failure or disappointment. So below we will talk about a tool to deal with disappointment while in movement.

Below is my three-day process for Dealing with pain, strife and disappointment. Let something go wrong in my life whether it's in a relationship or rather my plans just didn't go the way I expected, this is my process. I give myself three days to go through this process. I'll acknowledge the initial blow but I press through my emotions towards it and figure out how to move from there.

3-day method.

Day 1 is the initial blow.. take it in. Cry, be hurt, feel that pain, sulk. **(Write down what hurt you)**

Day 2 **Process it.** Analyze, look at all the elements of whatever has happened, what's good out of it. Acknowledge the bad as well **(How did that make you feel? Be brutally honest, Pick 2 completely different people to talk to and express these raw feelings after you talk to God. Take in their opinions with an open mind)**

Day 3 **What's next?** You've been hurt, you've processed now it's time to move. You can't stay in that same place. **(What is the next move? How will you move to pass this hurt? How will you refocus yourself?)**

Wilderness (The Wait)

A season of solitude is not rare. Sometimes God can't get to you in crowds. The Key is staying encouraged during those lonely seasons.

The biggest lesson I've learned in seasons of loneliness is that it is extremely uncomfortable. I found myself in this season a couple of times and neither time has been easier than the other. I've gone through seasons where God physically removes me from everybody. I've also been in situations where God called me to solitude in the midst of being around people that were closest to me. I can honestly say that one might be the harder of the two because the type of friend I have been made me very dependent on them emotionally for support. So when God started speaking to me about certain things that didn't require my friendships it started to make me uncomfortable. But I started to realize there were certain things that I had to go through that my friends couldn't go through with me. That was not to say that I was leaving their lives or them leaving mine, but that I was separating, for now, to prepare for my season of elevation. When you are waiting for a harvest to come it can be very nerve-wracking. You could do everything that you normally do right for your crop to come in. But sometimes it doesn't come or you can have a parasite that you are not used to having or even another animal that you've never encountered. The weather could change and smother your seed and the crazy thing is all of these things are completely out of your control. So it's your job in this season to practice patience. Understand the value of movement in his perfect peace or being still in His perfect peace. Trust that the harvest is protected and that every method he's given you to see these seeds grow will work. Know that you have planted your seed in good ground and you just have to keep watering them. Keep pouring and praying over them. Keep working on finding other things to do that can strengthen your crop... until you see it break ground.

Prosperity

Know that you will reap what you sow.

God will not leave you in one season. You can delay the process but he has set out the path. Your ability to get to what he has promised you is connected to your obedience and discipline.

Lesson Learned

Once I started to understand that life moves in seasons, I stopped being surprised at hardships. My perception of hard times became just as valuable as my perception of good times. Each Good time is supposed to be better than the last. But that betterment comes from the lesson that you get in those bad times. The devil that you fought in the last season was only an object he wasn't the lesson. He was the sharpener of the tools that you would eventually need in your next season but the lesson is you learning how to use these newly sharpened tools. So once I started connecting the two I learned how to endure each season differently. Each season will require a different version of you. Once you understand this about your personal seasons, you'll begin to understand yourself better. Not only just yourself in regular but yourself in battle form. Knowing the difference between these two people will show which person thrives in whatever season you are in. Because some seasons are going to require battle and others will require mental and strategic you. It's like knowing the game of boxing and how you need to physically have a strategy that fits the fighter you are but combats your enemy and their weaknesses, but also having the mental strength of a chess player. Both require a strategy but they require a different type of person to walk that strategy out.

7

Not The Same

They didn't tell us

When you start in a pack you don't always finish that way.

Your path is your path

God knows your destination even if you can't see the road

Failure is always an option, in fact, it's part of the process

Sometimes you don't reap from the seeds you sow in the season you are currently in.

1st Quarter- Stay in the Game

I was in middle school. We won back-to-back championships and I was arguably one of the best female players coming out of middle school that year. But the problem was I had a lot of weight on me. I was playing point guard then had to move back to the post in 8th grade. At this time middle school basketball was serious like high school basketball. High schools would come to our games to "scout". The competition at that time was crazy. I remember no schools really wanted me and I think it was more because of my size and weight. My best friend at the time was like 6 feet since we were in the sixth grade so everybody wanted her. Coach Shaw took us to tryouts for the crossovers and we both ended up making the team but my best friend stayed and I ended up leaving probably not even a month later. This connection with the crossovers eventually led to her going to King High School.

During this time you had to take a test to get into the Cass, King, and Renaissance and I didn't pass the test. Since I didn't pass the test and neither of these schools was really checking for me as far as ball. I really didn't know where I was going to school. Crockett high school was right up the street from my middle school and I had a good relationship with the high school coach and it wasn't far so this was the only school in the city that my mom was considering letting me go to. But one of my teammates from my seventh-grade year who was a really close friend of mine actually had moved to Warren and then somehow or another she ended up moving back to the city and she moved around the corner from where I was staying. I went to the park one day and I ran into her older brother. I was so excited because she was literally like one of my best friends and when she left the school I was hurt and she was one of my favorite players to play with. So when I saw her brother I instantly was like "Where is she at?". It just so happened she was around the corner. We ended up linking up and she invited me to open a gym at Fitzgerald. I had never in my life even ever heard of Fitzgerald so this was something that I kind of brushed off and eventually she ended up telling the head coach about me. Later on, he and his daughter came to one of my games for middle school and we met at the game where afterward he ultimately extended the invite for me to come to an open gym as well. I'll never forget that interaction with Kristian for the first time, who would end up being my point guard there. She was also his daughter. She was really excited about me and that gave me a lot of confidence because like I said I just didn't feel like anybody wanted me so my confidence was shot. I was very self-conscious about my weight so running into somebody who really wanted me was really a boost that I needed. I was really starting to believe that I wouldn't get the chance to play high school ball, at least not with the good schools because nobody was messing with me.

Now I didn't live in the district for Fitzgerald so I had to test in as a School of Choice Student. I ended up passing the test to get into there, now ain't that crazy. I couldn't pass the test to get into the schools that I thought I wanted to be in. Most of my close friends went to one of the three, none of them had a problem passing the test and I was sick that the plan to be with some of them didn't work out. But this was ordained by God, in fact, everything that happened for me from that point of leaving middle school was literally step-by-step the plan God had for my life. Even when I tried to stray away from it he literally lays out a plan and it will come to pass no matter what happens no matter what trials or injuries I would deal with.

Fast forward now I'm at Fitzgerald as a freshman. We came in with a team full of freshman sophomores, one junior, and two seniors. We would go on to win the school's first conference in 70 years, the first district ever, and earned our first Regional appearance. We would go on to win two more districts during my time while being there. During the four years of my being in high school, we got three districts, three regional appearances, and brought home four conference championships. Most of the girls that I ended up playing with during my time of being there we were together for the first 3 years and we played in the summer together so our relationship grew very strong, which reflected on the court. A lot of those girls I am still extremely close to. But even with all of that success, what people don't tell you about sports especially at the high school level is when you start to prepare for college they don't tell you how recruiting is when you are trying to get to the next level.

Now at this point, I need us to understand a few things. I had a lot of success as an athlete. I had won championships in middle school. I had gotten some districts. I had become a three-sport athlete at this time playing soccer, swimming, and basketball. Basketball had been such a major part of my life for so long I started wanting to know who I was outside of basketball. Now the thing with this is just like any other teenager I started rebelling against the plan that God had laid out. I thought I could get to my destination based on the work that I had already done and then after my junior season we went undefeated and ended up losing in the district championship. So after that year I honestly felt like I had kind of solidified who I was as a player and I would just choose when these offers started rolling in. This is how simple I was thinking things would go so my focus started to be somewhere else. That was literally just the beginning of my story but me just being an arrogant teenager led to starting to do my own thing apart from God's plan. I started not training every summer like I normally do. I never took the summer off until this moment heading into my senior year which was probably hands-down the worst time to take a break from training. I wasn't playing AAU. I didn't train as I should've. I went to a leadership camp for the student council. I just wanted to see myself in other lights that didn't involve basketball so that's what I did. The problem is God had woven himself into my situation and basketball was a big part of what he was getting ready to do for me. So when I decided to stray away from that plan it started creating some friction in my process and then it started revealing to me things that I wouldn't understand because I hadn't gone through them yet.

So the result of me taking the summer off was me coming back into my senior season completely out of shape. Now the team that we had just went undefeated with and had a great season with, most of that team was seniors so they were gone. This was supposed to be my year, but instead, I came back completely out of shape. My little sister Ree-Ree ended up having to carry us in the first 10 games. I remember our season being 20+ games. The first 10 games were the first half of the season and my sister was playing her tail off. She was playing most of the minutes in the game, she was averaging dang near 30pts a game. She was trying to will us and I think we might've gone five and five the first 10 games. But in the midst of her playing so hard and me being so out of shape and not being able to produce her body started breaking down. I remember my coach being so mad at me because he knew I wasn't who I was supposed to be. I literally got cussed out every single game and every practice. I would have to stay over extra in practice to run because he was trying to get me in shape. In the midst of all the fussing at the time of course I had a complete attitude because I was a snotty teenager. But the reality of what was going on with me was I had fallen out of love with basketball. My spiritual life was nonexistent and I just wanted to know myself. None of these things were gonna get me to the place that I had set goals to go. So my coach being who he was like I said I had to stay over. I always had two extra of whatever we were doing. He pulled a drastic move and sat my sister for like three games. He didn't play her because she was cramping so bad in her legs from playing so much and so hard. He told me I could either get it together or my senior season can go down the drain. With my back against the wall and the fear of disappointing not only my teammates but my little sister in particular because she was playing so hard and I hated to see her hurt like that I began to pull it together. So a couple of things happened at this moment. He developed a work ethic in me because he demanded more out of me when I couldn't demand it out of myself. Then within about three weeks, I started seeing myself as myself again on the court. My emotions and going through an identity crisis literally almost cost me my career and the thing that would eventually pay for me to go to school. So now I'm in shape.

A quick recap of where we are right now. I've gone through 4 years of high school. I had an identity crisis where I was ready to step away from the goal for a second because I thought I had enough to get my offers. I've had the battle back from being out of shape to get in shape for my team so mentally I had to get myself in a good headspace so I've had my first battle with myself. God had sent me a friend that spiritually helped me refocus as my coach mentally strengthened me. I did not know everything that I went through in that short amount of time was for a reason. I was seeing what I was going to need for the next six months for what was getting ready to happen during my senior season and my freshman year of college.

Now I've gone through my complete senior season I have no offers on the table, the only interest I have is the head coach from Schoolcraft community college. This was a good thing because Schoolcraft had just won a national championship for community college so it was a great opportunity but something happened and it was from this point that everything in my life began to change with my perception of basketball and how tangible I was. With only Schoolcraft on the table, the coach was very active in recruiting me. I still love her to this day. Her personality was absolutely amazing but I was trying to hold out and see if I could get some more options. So my school ended up hosting a second chance game. This is where kids who didn't have any offers play in a game in front of college coaches as the last opportunity to see the recruiting daylight. So I'm playing in this game and I was having a great game too. I got the rebound and spent time trying to drive baseline. I went one way and turned back the other way trying to get past the defender and I and the defender ended up going head to head. The collision was so loud like literally you could hear everybody in the gym gasp for air when we collided. Now my forehead went into her eye so every-body was paying her attention and I'm telling everybody I'm OK. So I came to the bench, and my coach asked me if I was good. I'm like I'm good and he subs me back into the game. I'm going into the game and I started dribbling in the wrong direction. Instantly my mom is yelling from the bleachers to get me out of the game. I left the game and my mom took me home. Before we left the trainer at the game looked me over and told my mom If I continued to have a headache, to take me to the emergency room. They feared that I could have a concussion. Long story short I ended up being in the hospital for three days with a con-cussion. Now here's the thing. Up until this point, I hadn't heard any-thing other than a couple of sprained ankles, maybe a hyperextended knee, nothing major as far as injuries. So I ended up going through this and making the decision to go to Northwood University instead of the Juco. I took some pressure from my mom about the decision and still to this day I think God was trying to teach me to make choices on my own about my future in that situation. But being a first-generation graduate I valued my mom's opinion so I went with what would make her happy instead of myself.

As I am recovering from the concussion I couldn't work out I couldn't really train the way I wanted to because of headaches so it kind of put my recruiting at a standstill. I need you all to understand some-thing. Specifically, young kids who are preparing for college, I need you to understand that your decision about school is YOUR decision. I was in a good position where I could've gone to this community college, did two years of my years at one of the top junior colleges in the coun-try, and been about my way. But then I wouldn't have this story to tell this advice to give in this moment so I don't regret my past but I just need you to understand it as a child going through this process this is YOUR process. What I learned is you can't take your advice from peo-ple who haven't been down the road that you are trying to go down. It's no disrespect but nobody in my family other than my older cousin who was playing overseas at the time went to college on a basketball scholarship. So I was literally going through the situation blind. I had been this great student in school and I was this great athlete and I honestly believed that because of what I had accomplished in high school that choosing a college wouldn't have been so complicated. I believe my mother felt like I was too good for a community college. So we battled about that decision for months and she talked me into going to Northwood and I really didn't wanna go and the plan was for me to go to Northwood and work on the basketball team.

Free Game: Your financial aid will cover those two years of Community College. The same classes you take your first two years of that expensive 4-year college are the same classes you will take at a Community college. Community college is always a way for you to take more time to develop as a player and learn how to be a college athlete.

2nd Quarter

Here I was making a deal with my mom to go to Northwood and what was leftover in my tuition they would have to pay out of pocket. I was so new to this process I let so many outside entities interfere with my decision. What they don't tell you is when you come from the hood and you are you good at a sport and you go to school and your hood sees the potential in you, that comes with pressure. Not even necessarily pressure from people but the pressure from those expectations of those people. Not only do they expect the hood baby to push through and rep for the neighborhood but you get pressure from your family. Like I said when you are the first for a lot of things that pressure comes naturally cause your family starts seeing you as like a savior. They start seeing you as the pinnacle of the potential of "Getting out". They start making comments like, " She gonna get is out of here" or "She gonna

make sure we all good". All of those things influenced my actual decision and ultimately I ended up going to Northwood University.

   At this point, I turn on my intentions to tryouts once I make it to
campus. My try-out was set for the second or third week of September so I hit the ground running. I started working out every day from
swimming, shooting and running. I was getting to it on all levels. The
concussion thing I felt had me starting a step behind so I was trying
my best to get in the best shape possible. So at this point, I'm trying to
make up for lost time grinding it out. I couldn't get on the same page
with the girls who were already on the team to play at the open gym so
eventually, I started playing it at the open gym with the boy's basketball
team and the football players. I had begun to develop a reputation with
the male athletes because they were playing with me. Well, one particular night in early September I got a phone call about a little guy who
was like a little brother to me, he had been killed. So that weekend or
the following one I went home for the funeral. I came back to school
on September 21 which is actually his birthday. I was extremely emotional so I decided to go and play in an open gym. I was playing great
and was ready to leave. The guys begged me to play one last game so I
stayed and did. Literally, on the last bucket, they threw me the ball on
a fast break, I was by myself, I took my first step for my layup and my
left knee hybrid extended backward. It pops out of place really hard and
then it pops back forward and I instantly hit the ground screaming. The
guys start running over to me and asking if I'm OK and I'm just screaming. I remember opening and closing my leg trying to tell myself that I
was OK but my leg was completely numb. At the time I had fallen out
with my roommate so I couldn't call her and ask her to take me to the
hospital. A guy I went to high school who was up there playing football, I called him. He was in the film so he couldn't take me. I'll never
forget this girl named Taryn called my RA so that she could drive me
to the hospital. Taryn went with me.

   By the time I got to the hospital, my knee was the size of my head and if you know me you know I don't have a small head. I had a team-mate who tore her ACL twice in high school so I kind of had come to the conclusion of what was going on but I tried to give myself some hope. They put me in a straight leg cast and gave me some pain meds. They sent me home and remembered getting to my dorm and I was in so much pain. I couldn't sleep and I was so upset I cried for hours. Then when I finally was able to go to sleep I woke up at about 5 a.m. and started throwing up everywhere because the pain medicine that they gave me was extremely strong and I had nothing on my stomach. My roommate at the time helped clean up my throw-up. After she cleaned up my throw up she helped me get ready to get in the shower I got ready for class and she left. I never saw her in that room again after that. So now I don't have a roommate. I'm just in a room by myself. Taryn would stop by my room now and then to help me to the cafe. I remember calling home and telling my mom and fam that I was going to stick the semester out and to just be patient. I called and made my appointment for my knee and I had already talked to my RA about taking me to the appointment.

So I called my mom and I told her my plans. About two or three hours after I got off the phone with my mom, my aunt called my grandmother and told her "No, we're going to go get her tonight". So my grandmother calls me at about 9 p.m. and tells me, "OK we just got on the road we bought to come to get you please pack as much stuff as you can". My aunt said that my great-grandmother came to her in a dream. She tried to lay back down after my mom told her what was going on with me. She said my great-grandma came to her and told her, "Go get my Baby". So about 3 a.m., my aunt and Grandma drove up. With my grandma and me on crutches and in a straight leg cast, we packed my whole dorm up in a Ford Fusion. Everything except for my clothes in my closet and moved back home that night. Now I'm feeling like a complete failure. Like I didn't accomplish what I was supposed to accomplish and I'm hurt. I'm not about to be able to play for a full year. This injury literally happened two days before I was getting ready to have my try-out for the team. I knew I was gonna make the team, that wasn't my concern but I also knew that I really didn't want to be at the school but I was just trying to make the best of the situation. I decided I was gonna work hard no matter what. Now I'm in a situation where I'm hurt and I'm at a place I really don't want to be and I'm still trying to just stick it out and that just wasn't God's plan. Truthfully the pressures of being the one in my family are what was driving me. I felt like a failure when I had to come home because I felt like I let a lot of people down. A lot of people expected me to do a lot of great things and not only am I not able to do those things even at this level but I'm not able to do them at all. That's a lot of pressure on an 18-year-old. That's a lot for an 18-year old that's dealing with a major injury to process. I was so young I really didn't know how to deal with it.

So ultimately I ended up having to drop out of school. After getting kidnapped in the middle of the night I remember getting to my grandmother's house and my granddad butch meeting us at the door. They got me all setup. He already had the front room set up for me. I stayed with my grandmother and my grandfather for my whole recovery process. My mom called to schedule my appointments and everything the next couple of days and in my head like I said I knew I was hurt like I knew it was my ACL. I just was trying so hard to not accept it. In fact, I reached out to Schoolcraft coach to find out that she was no longer head coach but she put me in contact with the assistant coach was not a hair coach and I told him the situation and they were both interested in me so he told me to come up to register for school probably I'm a say two weeks after the initial injury. After running around trying to find a doctor and having to switch hospitals, finally, the DMC (Detroit Medical Center) took me on as a patient. My absolutely amazing doctor, would not allow me to have surgery until I did rehab first. Now as an athlete this irritated me because that means this was slowing up my process for me to potentially be able to get back to playing basketball. But in his mind, he was telling me that if I'm able to walk normally and get a lot of the swelling and strength and stuff back before having surgery my recovery would be that much easier after surgery.

After my first doctor visit, he literally started me in rehab the same day and at this point, my knee is still swollen really bad I couldn't fully bend it. I couldn't put any weight on it so the first goal was to be able to fully bend at 90° and straighten it completely. My initial tear was September 21st, I didn't have surgery until November 13th. When I tell you I was so frustrated every time I went into rehab or every time I had a doctor's appointment. I'm thinking this is gonna be the day I get my surgery date. I'm thinking this is going to be the day that I know how close I am to being able to get back to the thing that I love. Every single time I got disappointed. It got to the point where my last couple of visits I stopped even asking about the surgery date. I just would go in and get ready for rehab after my visit. I told my mind to just focus on rehab, focus on the process. Eventually, he gave me a surgery date.

Half time

I'm gonna take this halfway point to express some things that I learned during this time about myself and about the process of being an athlete. The first thing that no one tells you about being an athlete is the mental strain on you after you get injured. Everybody is in support of you when you are high. But those late nights when you can't sleep because you're in pain, those moments where you can't go to the gym and work out to relieve stress because you can't walk, that's a different kind of loneliness. When you use to be independent and you're not able to do those things or move at your own will that is a hard thing to process, let alone the injury itself. The game being taken away from you is a small issue compared to the mental battles that you begin to have when you are completely shut down from playing a sport. The value of that sport to your psyche is almost equal to the air you breathe and the water you drink. It's that important to you when you decide that this is something that you really want to do. The reason I say this is because if you mentally don't handle the injury properly you'll never come back from it. You may physically be OK but mentally you'll never get back to the place you were and that's the other thing that as an athlete you need to know. Your initial goal is not to get back to where you were before the injury. Your goal is to get better than what you were because the place that you were in is what got you injured. The things that you were doing or not doing in that particular season of your life as an athlete is what got you injured. So now you have to learn the better technique of running and now you have to learn the better technique of living. You learn how Important lifting and other aspects of your nutrition are. You understand how important taking care of your body is versus the sport itself. Once you learn how to take care of your body the game is going to come but you have to learn how to take care of yourself because if your body is taken care of it allows you to play the sport. Then your mind is gonna be taken care of and you can accelerate in anything you wanna do. Your body does exactly what your mind tells it to do so if both of those things are in a healthy place you getting into a better space as an athlete is going to be second nature.

3rd Quarter Failure or correction?

After having surgery I went on a long process of recovery. I'm really grateful to this day for the team at DMC. I had three different physical therapists and they were all amazing and they were all I needed for every different day that I was there during my rehab. In the midst of my rehab, I was getting stronger and just like a mom, she noticed it so she sent me outside to rake leaves lol. At the time I had talked to the Schoolcraft coach but I just didn't get a vibe from him that Schoolcraft was the fit for me anymore. I was still attending Schoolcraft for classes. Schoolcraft was 35-40 minutes away from my house. I was driving to school on crutches. I'm going to school and I'm mentally trying to prepare myself to go into another situation that I'm not even comfortable with because I'm not really comfortable with the coach. But this day I was out raking the leaves my old position coach from high school Coach Brown pulled up on me. She knew I had this surgery. She asked me how I was doing and she asked me about school. I explained to her the situation at Schoolcraft and before I could truly get what was going on out of my lips she stopped me and was like "Have you signed anything for Schoolcraft?" and I told her no. She told me not to because Wayne County was getting their program back and she wanted to build around me. So just because of the history we had and what she was to me in high school this was a no-brainer decision to make. It was a no-brainer although I talked to my family and they couldn't understand why I was getting ready to go to this school that had such a bad reputation.

A lot of people who don't know, Wayne County at the time was like the lowest of low on the totem pole as far as community college was concerned. I didn't even think about it when I made the decision. It just felt right. So signing day came up and I remember going through months of rehab not hearing from Schoolcraft's coach and then literally the day before signing day he reached out to me and at that point I had decided to sign in Wayne County. I explained that the decision was off the strength of me and this coach already having a relationship and it was just more convenient for me. So I got to Wayne County and I hit the ground running. When preseason started I wasn't able to start my first couple of weeks because I was still in rehab but once I got released coaches didn't hold up on me. The first year at Wayne County I definitely think was a learning year for me. Injuries change you as a player so my mentality wasn't the same. I was stronger mentally but now my idea of the game had changed. I had to change how I approached the game. A lot of the things that I used to do I changed like I didn't do a lot of banging, I didn't do a lot of unnecessary movements. All that sounds fine and dandy but the reality of the situation is I was terrified of getting hurt again so mentally that showed in my game. My first year was not terrible but it definitely wasn't what it could've been.

After the first season, I spent the whole summer mentally trying to get myself stronger. I knew I was OK. I just needed it to get in better shape and it just came when we were playing basketball more, not so much working out. I don't think people understand the only true way to get in basketball shape is to play basketball because no workout is giving you the stop-and-go motion of the actual game. So that summer I spent a lot of time just playing basketball. It seemed like every time I played in the summer I was getting better and better so by the time pre-season started I looked great and I had lost a lot of weight. My second year ended up being probably one of the best years of basketball I've played in my whole life. We had a lot of struggles that year as a team off the court with teammates quitting. We ended up finishing the season with six girls and I ended up coming off the bench as a part of a strategy to get some firepower coming into the game. Coach decided on a game plan to get some of my teammates an opportunity to get going and then follow up with me so I had to accept it. Now let me tell you, at this particular time I'm averaging a double-double. I'm top 25 in the region and my coach came to me about coming off the beach. Now, this is for my athletes, especially the athletes in this generation who are bred in entitlement. Sometimes you have to make decisions that are best for your team in order for y'all to be successful, it's not really about you. I think one of the things that has made me successful as a player and have made my career last as long as it has is the fact that I was very unselfish on and off the court. My main objective was to win. It didn't have anything to do with scoring or none of that.

At the end of my sophomore season, I had won every award that you could win on a junior college level individually except All American. The only reason I believe I didn't win the All-American is that our record was bad. We still ended up going to the final four that year though. My coaches kind of made it a big deal, I on the other hand was in awe because I never really got individual awards. I remember being at our banquet at the end of the year and I broke down crying as they started naming off all of the awards I had received. I hadn't ever hit that kind of success as an individual and after an injury like the one I had gone through it meant the world to me. This gave me validation that I was good like I knew I was good but this was me seeing all my hard work pay off. I came back from a rough injury, I graduated with a 3.5 and I gave my team everything I had every night. I knew how hard I worked to get to that point so my emotions took over and I just enjoyed the moment.

But then we do know that wherever there is sunshine there is rain. I remember our first round of playoffs we played Mott Community College and this is our second year in a row playing them first game. I was starting to get sick as we were going into the playoffs. So I remember the first half of this game feeling extremely sluggish but I knew this was a big first game. I remember coming out of the locker room and one of the assistant coaches from the other team looked at me and she was like "hey where are you going to school? ", I felt ashamed that again I had to tell someone I didn't know where I was going. I remember coming out of high school I didn't have any offers and I honestly believe I just didn't handle recruitment properly which nobody had taught me how. I was the first one in my family to go through this process. So I found myself literally in the same position all over again after having a breakout year and being one of the top forwards in the region in community college that year.

We ended up winning that game but lost to St. Clair in the final four. I had a great game but I had pneumonia while playing so it was a good but rough game. After the game was over now the real game was starting. Now I have to deal with the fact that I'm not recruited. At the time our men's team had won everything and were getting ready to go to the national tournament. So the guy who was in charge of making highlight tapes for our program was more focused on the men's team because it was more likely that we had more men than women trying to go to the next level. As I said we finished the season with six girls so literally I was like one of the only girls who was trying to go and play ball and he just wasn't messing with me like that, my highlights just were not a priority. I just remember working so hard that summer. From waking up early in the morning for workouts to running hills I just wanted to stay ready no matter what happened. I had no clue where I was going to school, I just knew I was going to school. This grit and focus were established in high school. That time when my coach ran me extra because I didn't do my part, that moment prepared me for this. My family supported me and with that support and always having access to a gym I knew I just had to keep working. I and my assistant coach worked that whole summer. I remember having long talks with him and just when I was starting to get discouraged, he would speak life into me. Closer to the end of the summer I still didn't have any offers so one day Coach J went to church and the young lady that went to his church was an alumnus of The Tennessee State University. He told his young lady my situation and told her what was going on with me. So she ended up taking his word and making a Facebook post about me. After her Facebook posts, she had a couple of coaches reach out to her asking for film. Of course, I didn't have it because of the situation with our film man. My head coach from Juco was going through a transition from coach to coach at a high school and also the Athletic Director there. I remember driving up to the school and sitting in her office for like three hours trying to pick out my film from the last couple of years. When I went home I had his old desktop Computer at my grandmother's house. I wasn't even sure if it was gonna work but I had to figure something out. I had an iPhone at the time, I downloaded a stop and go app and I watched all of the films and wrote down the times where I knew I was doing something I needed to be on the film. I created my own highlight tape using an app and my iPhone and literally, you can hear my dog barking in the background.

So after I make this tape and send it to Coach, the lady she posted it and I kid you not about two weeks later Coach J called and asked me, "So what do you think about Tennessee?", and I was like "huh? What about Tennessee? I don't know anything about it". He was like "Nah I'm talking about to live", we both kinda started laughing on the phone because I'm so confused. Eventually, I started putting two and two together. I had an offer from a school in Tennessee. He explained to me the situation and told me he had just talked to the head coach and that he was offering a full ride. He gave him my number so a call would be coming in soon. About five minutes into my and Coach J conversation Coach Lew from Cumberland University was calling my phone. I could hear the excitement in his voice. He told me how he loved my highlight tape. He started laughing talking about my dog in the background. He told me what he was trying to build and how many transfers and everything he was coming in and talked to me a little bit about the school and told me that he wanted to pay for everything and I truly was speechless. Literally like I said at the time I didn't have a clue where I was going to school but I kept working. I watched my faith grow, from going through the injury to pressing through the situation that no one was recruiting me. I just was pressing and trusting God in the midst. Sure enough, he came through.

I got off the phone and I cried like a baby. I cried harder than when I found out I won individual awards. I cried harder than I cried when I tore my ACL. I knew what I had gone through to get to this point of hearing my first offer. I hadn't accepted anything, I hadn't seen the school, but I was just so relieved and so happy that my hard work had paid off. I was starting to see the light at the end of the tunnel. Now if I could enter here for a second of advice I would tell people when you go onto your process and you start seeing a light at the end of the tunnel and even when you get to the light know that it's another tunnel coming. Understand that there is another valley coming, you don't learn how to get the strength to tackle the next high if you don't go through a low point.

So sure enough about a week or so later Coach Lew started emailing me, sending me the info for my visit. He set the schedule for when I would arrive and sent me my flight information. His assistant coach Coach Moore contacted me every single day. She sent me a summer work out and she would check on me every day. One day I got on Twitter and I usually don't get on Twitter. I checked my inbox and I saw an inbox from a young lady who attended Tuskegee University. She told me that her coach had been looking for me for months. She gave me her coach info and told me to call them. Long story short I ended up getting my second offer from Tuskegee University a week before I left for my first official visit. So the plan was for me to schedule my visit to Tuskegee when I came back from Cumberland. Once I got to Tennessee I loved the coaches because all of them were young. I made it through the visit and had already made up my mind that I would sign there. Coach Lew gave me my letter of Intent to take back home so that I could sign with my family and friends. I remember getting on the plane with this envelope in my hand and I was tripping out. I really got a scholarship in my hand. I just felt so accomplished. I think I cried like the whole flight home.

I came home and told my family and athletic department the news. They planned my signing day. The good part was my best friend Q had just signed to a school in Tennessee a couple of weeks before so it was dope we would be in the same state. Everything's great. But Tuskegee never stopped calling.

Free Game

Always be honest during your recruitment process not only be honest with other people but also be honest with yourself.

1.) Know the type of student you are.

2.Know what you're looking for in a school because that's the key to you playing a sport. If you're not gonna be successful in the classroom then the sport is not gonna matter. I wasn't a big campus type of person. A lot of people saw me as a D1 player but I knew I wasn't. I had to figure out what works for me and I truly believe Cumberland was the best fit for me.

Now, most kids with multiple offers on the table of course they gonna go visit each one. But I was just honest with myself. I knew I had already decided so it wasn't a point for me to waste the other school's time. I kid you not because I handled the situation properly years after I made the decision the coach still would mess with me. *To the kids, never burn any bridges, you never know what could happen so always handle situations properly so that you can go to these people if you ever get in a jam. I got down in Tennessee and I've never been happier just cause I feel like I'm finally laying some groundwork for myself. But all the things I went through that situation could've went sour quick. The way I handle Tuskegee I would've still had that opportunity on the table if things didn't work out.*

4th Quarter Passion or Purpose?

I got down to Tennessee and started showing my tail. My first couple opened gyms, nobody could do anything with me. I remember Pace, who was our other coach putting on her shoes to come out and check me. I was honored because this was who my coach compared me to. When I got there I had some pretty big shoes to fill and I honestly don't think I ever filled them but I got a great friendship out of the situation so it was cool. But we went through an open gym for about two weeks and I'm having a great experience here. The week before our first official practice at an open gym I tweaked my knee and this is the knee that I hurt years earlier. I didn't get to practice my first two or three weeks of practice because I was in rehab. I had to pretty much sit down and rest. It irritated me because it was messing up my rhythm and I wasn't gonna be able to jump right into building chemistry with my team. Due to the fact I wasn't on the floor as much, I found myself having a hard time retaining the plays. It frustrated the hell out of me because I had never had that issue before. But thankfully my Asst. Coaches and my teammates were a really big help in that area. My head coach literally never saw me healthy. Like from the moment he saw my highlights he didn't see me healthy until probably the last like 10 games of my senior season. This was my first bout with the injury bug here at Cumberland. It kind of just got worse from that moment on.

I started the season initially as a starter. I think the first two games I still started even with the injury but eventually, I lost my starting spot. I couldn't keep up due to the injury I was dealing with and that was a reality check for me. I felt like I worked so hard but at this point, I'm battling my body. I started feeling like I was losing because my body is not responding the way I needed to respond for me to play the way that I need to play. So boom I've lost my spot. I can't get mad at the coach. I'm not producing what I should be on the floor so I have to go with whatever his plan is and whenever my number is called I'll be ready. Although I had lost my spot I was still the first sub off the bench for my position so I couldn't be too upset. Just like my Sophomore year when my coach decided to have me coming off the bench, I feel like God had prepared me mentally for this moment. I've never been much of an angry athlete or angry person for that matter so I took it for what it was. We go through a couple of games and we get to about the third game. We go to Middle Georgia. Our athletic trainer at the time was gone with our soccer team to nationals so we didn't have a trainer with us but Middle Georgia did. Somehow or another this girl tried to take charge on me but she jumped and when she jumped I just knew I was about to draw the foul, so I leaned into her. Her mouth was open, she came down and her tooth got stuck in the bridge of my nose. So I touched my face immediately it just felt like a lot of pressure in my face. But even with the pressure I remember walking back to the bench being more mad because the ref called a charge on me instead of a foul on her lol. I sat the rest of the game and we ended up losing. My nose bled dang near the whole way back to campus and I just knew I was about to sit out some games.

So what I need us to understand is at this point I had only been at school for like three or four months and I've had two injuries that have sat me down so that's the thing, if I could give any advice to athletes man it's just understand that things can go completely wrong quickly. At this point you could've never told me like that I was getting ready to keep having to go through this. So I finally got over the concussion I'm starting to play, starting to get in a little bit in shape. A couple of games go by and my minutes are going up. I'm still not really productive yet because I'm trying to find my way on the court but I'm there. In practice, we were running a new play and I was coming down the court. In my head, I'm like dang I'm supposed to go to the set a pick over there. But the problem was my body was already going one way so I tried to turn in the midst of me running and turning and pop my ankle. I went down screaming and yelling and my ankle was in excruciating pain. I'm thinking this is a sprained ankle and that's what it was. But it was bad enough that I'm not able to practice. I actually got put in a boot for a little while because the sprain was so bad. I played through it and then I started to kind of get my feet under me. The game right before it was time for us to go on winter break we were away. I remember getting off the bus and the side of my foot was hurting. It wasn't so much my ankle anymore so I told my trainer and she looked concerned. When the game was over she said, "OK, you got two options. You can get the x-ray now and could potentially be some bad news and it's gonna hold you up from going home or I can put you in a boot now and we do the x-ray when you come back". So I decided to go with the second option.

When I went back to school I got my x-ray. Now the new battle was a sprained ankle turned stress fracture in my foot. Now it's really just a crack in your bone. It's not a complete break so the doctor gave me a choice of sitting out and being done for the rest of the season or I could play the rest of my season. But If I played I would have to be in a boot every moment that I wasn't on the court. At the time our starting big who took my spot was out because of grades for the rest of the season. I knew deep in my heart we had this goal to get to the national tour-

nament so I looked at my doctor and assistant coach and told them I
wanted to play. I didn't think we would make the national tournament
if I didn't and that's not to me being cocky or me saying I was this or
that because at the time I wasn't even really producing any points. But
I knew what I brought to the table as a player. I knew I could give us
something even if it wasn't a lot it would be enough to get us to the
goal or at least close. So that was the decision, I would play and when
I was off the court I had to be in a boot. I got through the season and
we made it to the national tournament and the last game in which we
ended up getting eliminated, I completely broke my foot. The crazy
thing was before the game, the warm-up, and the practice the day before I felt great like I didn't feel any pain. I knew I was gonna have to
have surgery and I just didn't know what my future was holding for the
next season.

A couple of weeks down the line my coach talked with my assistant
coach. He concluded that he wanted to give me a medical redshirt for
my senior year. This medical redshirt would allow me to sit for a year.
I would still be on scholarship but it would allow me the time to let my
body heal for me to be able to play a healthy senior season. I was super ecstatic when he called me into the office and told me what his plan
was and I just knew this was gonna work. I was going to finally have a
chance to get healthy and be the asset I knew I could be. This was God,
I just knew this was God making everything work out for My good.
My coach told me that he did not want me to work out. He wanted me
to take the time to go to rehab and heal and allow my body to rest for
the whole summer. So for the first time since I had a midlife crisis in
high school, I took a summer off. The problem was by the time the fall
hit and we were maybe two weeks away from school starting my coach
called me back into his office. He then informed me that he wouldn't be
able to sit me as planned due to a technicality with my eligibility. See in
NAIA your eligibility is based on how many full-time semesters you've
been in school. Now when I saw my ACL I was enrolled in Northwood
as a full-time student although I did not finish my time there that didn't

take away from the fact that I was a full-time student. Then I also did the whole semester at Schoolcraft and although I did not stay at school or play there it counted against me. Then I did two years at Wayne County so that's a total of three years which made me lose my extra year of eligibility.

So now I'm at this point where I don't have a choice but to play this season. My preseason starts like three weeks after school starts so now not only do I have to suck this situation up but I have to figure out how to get my body into basketball shape. I remember my assistant coach walking me out of the office into the gym on the side of the bleachers and just hugged me. She let me cry and she said: "OK you got time to cry now but after today we got to get to work". I couldn't run. I was still on crutches. I was actually in a boot but I wasn't allowed to run and I was barely walking and wasn't in two shoes. So I was feeling way behind because I didn't really do a lot of rehab over the summer of course because of what my coach requested. So in my head, I'm like but I don't know how in the hell I'm about to do this but I gotta figure it out. The next morning Coach Moore met me at the pool at 7 AM. I started in the pool getting extra work just trying to get some stamina and get my feet under me so when it was time for me to start rehab on land I wouldn't be so far behind.

I think God knew I was capable of coming back. I'm one of those people who perform better under pressure. My elementary coach used to tell us that pressure does two things: bust pipes or Make diamonds and it's up to you to determine which material you made out of. My back was against the wall I had to either put up or shut up. It didn't matter that time no longer was on my side, I had to make do with the time I had left. The crazy thing is heading into my senior year we got a new trainer also. Although my trainer my Junior year was great and went through every situation with me and patched me up the best she could, Solomon was different. I truly believe that this was God. God was telling me that "I got you, I know you weren't expecting this curveball but I need you to know that I got you and I will make sure you're straight". So now we grinding it out. Whenever I wasn't in the pool I was in the trainer's building getting treatment. When I was finally able to put two shoes on Coach P would come up late at night and rebound for me so I could get shots up. It was these moments with these Queens and Kings where I was able to be vulnerable in the midst of my pain and grind and they spoke life into me. They encouraged me more than I can ever explain during this time of my life. I didn't expect to play for at least the first couple of games of the season. My focus was getting ready for January. My coach wasn't rushing me but then something happened. I started to turn the corner. My mobility was getting better in practice. My limp was almost completely gone and I started being able to play longer without soreness once I got some inserts to lift my arch off the new screw that was in my foot. Needless to say, by the third game of the season I was ready. I wasn't ready in the sense that I was completely healthy but I was strong enough to play so he played me.

I was starting to get my feet under me and score a little bit more so my confidence was starting to come. By game five I was feeling myself again and it showed when we stepped into Lindsey Wilson gym that evening. We were going back-and-forth with this team. It was a great game. I was having a great game. I was standing on the side of the paint when my teammate Nicole drove in to the paint. The girl who was checking me stepped off me to try to take a charge on Nicole. I tried to backpedal out of the paint to get out of the way and somehow or another the girl who was checking me fell on the side of my knee. I heard a small pop. I get emotional talking about this specific event because I was so hurt. The screaming and yelling I did was more heartbreak than physical pain. I just knew I had torn my ACL again so that's more why I was screaming. My trainer gets to me and he's trying to calm down. When he finally got me up to walk on it I knew it wasn't my ACL, whew a sigh of relief but I also still knew something was wrong. He took me over to the training table and did the knee-jerking test that I absolutely hate. I told him where my pain was and he told me it sounds like my MCL. It was at that moment that I knew my basketball career was over. I had aspirations of going overseas and with my determination, I knew it was possible. I just knew I had to stay healthy. I just had to get through this year, get this weight off me, and get healthy but when I went down I accepted it. That was it.

I got on the bus called my old Asst. Coach told her what happened and asked her to pray for me. Then I called my family and told my mom and my dad. I told them I couldn't do this anymore. I cannot mentally come back from another injury like this. I'm exhausted. I can tell people how blessed I was to be able to go to college for free because of basketball. I can tell people how great of a college experience I had as an athlete. I can tell people the different places this game took me, the different people it brought into my life. But the very thing that I had given my all to was breaking me mentally and physically. I was being tested to my core and I couldn't figure out how many more tests I was gonna have to take before I could enjoy the game again. My passion was leaving because it was no longer my release, it was my stress. Then I started thinking about my future. I wanted to be able to play with my kids and not be full of aches and pains so soon. I felt like I had given everything I had in me to this game and it left me beaten with nothing but a degree to show for it.

Later I would go get an MRI and sure enough, I had a partial tear in my MCL. The doctor sat me down and told me my options were to sit out for the remainder of the season and hopefully after rehab will be back to the playoffs or I could just be done. So of course I decided I was gonna stick it out. I was hurt emotionally but if I knew this was going to be the end I wanted it to be on my terms and I wanted to be healthy ending it. Mentally I was tired from having to keep grinding to come back. I was tired from not being able to focus on other parts of my life and my college experience because I was always dealing with trying to heal from an injury. I was tired but mentally I was also at a peace. I was upset about the decision I had to make, I was upset at how I was forced to make it. I had a childhood dream that I was willing to chase and see all the way through but I also was in a place where I no longer felt like I had anything else to prove to myself when it came to this game. I think I have to credit this peace to my new involvement in my new church home as well. I had started going to church with Coach Moore and eventually ended up becoming a youth leader. This change in routine happened during the summer while I wasn't rehabbing. I didn't know at the time that the more involved in church and spending time serving and just being in God's presence that summer was preparing me for this moment. I spent a lot of time with Coach Moore that summer and it felt like I was in bible boot camp lol. A lot of worship, A lot of praying, A lot of church services. But I think this was God's intention because he knew this moment was coming. So because I had spent time with youth I felt like I started to see my purpose. I was at peace with letting my dream go. I started to understand that my dream was just a pit stop to my purpose so when it was time to give the ball up for good I was ok. I spent so much time worshiping and praising and in the church these things prepared me for when that "No " came. I had peace that wasn't given to me by the comfort of my friends or a significant other. That peace came from the only person that could comfort me as I prepared to separate from something that I thought was such a major part of who I was.

So on the road to "End it right" I sat the rest of the first half of the season. I did rehab twice a day and treatment 3 times a day on top of pool workouts for low-impact on my legs. I needed to get swelling out, get my range of motion back then get stronger. After we get it stronger we can focus on moving and putting pressure on the knee. This in-cluded jogging and small cuts all in a big bulky brace. I was so mad I had to play in this brace. My trainer pretty much told me I would finish my season in it and I assured him I wouldn't. I started off having to wear the brace in rehab, practices, and eventually when I would start play-ing again, in the games. With the routine I was in my legs was getting strong so fast I started being able to practice without the brace, but he would still make me play in the games with it. I was just focused on being productive whenever I was on the court. If I could give any advice again to athletes who may go through dealing with the injury bug, *my suggestion is to make sure that no matter what you are bringing something to the table, because of your injuries your flaws and everything is going wrong it's already on the table. You have a losing hand so make sure that when its your time whether it's 30 seconds, two minutes or five minutes that you make the best of the time and you give them everything that you absolutely can.* That's what I did when I was on the court. I may not have scored the most points. I may not have been the athlete I was when I was in junior college but I was productive. I was going to give you something whether it was energy, talking, or rebounding. Even if it was just encouragement for my team I was a piece of the puzzle that made sure I fit.

My trainer started seeing my progress and changed his thoughts. He then said he would expect me to be out of the brace by the time the conference tournament started. But we were in the middle of January and our Senior night was coming. I told God I did not want my family to come all the way down here and have to see me play in a brace so I needed to be out of it by then. So I told my trainer what I told God, he stuck to his timeline of Conference time lol. My trainer would take my brace home and wash it for me. He would bring it back for practice and games. But this one particular week which was about two weeks before the senior night, I started to bug him like I'm feeling good can we just take the brace off. He was like "No, you're not ready yet". We had a game in Alabama I believe. My assistant Coach P wasn't able to go but I remember our conversation when we left compared to when we came back. I remember telling her "like me and I feel good, like I haven't felt this good since I first got here". I was whining TO her because I wanted to come out of that brace so badly. My Trainer Solomon took my brace home and washed it. But when we got to the game and I came over to him to get it he went through his things only to discover he had accidentally left it at home. He just started shaking his head and laughing. He turned and looked at me and said, "Well I guess it's time for you to come out because tonight you don't have it". That night I think I scored My season-high in points. I also got a season-high in rebounds. I told him that God told me I wasn't gonna be in a brace for my whole season. He did not disappoint nor did he lie.

Postgame wrap up (Lessons Learned)

Going through my process of being an athlete was extremely strenuous but I also feel like it was not about me. I was the first in my family to go on a full scholarship and I had to make a lot of decisions being the first on my own. Everybody does not get paid to play college sports so if you do it's a blessing. But what they also don't tell you is that your preparation to becoming a college athlete is a lot bigger than what you do on the court or what you do on the field. What they don't tell you is that you are the package. If you don't put it together in a manner that benefits anybody or any program nine times out of 10 you are not going to play college sports. That package includes the sport, the classroom, and the way you carry yourself when out of the view of your authority figures. But I also feel like what they don't tell us is college is not always the route for everybody. I think our generation got caught up in the generation before us not seeking further education so they pushed us to further ours. But this was done with no plan or preparation. So what happened was a lot of us went to school unprepared, full of egos, full of childhood trauma, no order in our lives, no real support financially or emotionally. That is not beneficial to those who get the opportunity and then they look at us crazy when we end up back home. I feel like our generation owes the next everything. I think our generation is one of Enlightenment. We had to go through the mistakes and I think we see a lot of the stuff that was being drilled in us in the 90s was completely bull crap. It may have worked for some but for the most part, the formula that was drilled into us by the baby boomers no longer works for the world we currently live in.

The lessons I learned as an athlete we're pretty much simple perseverance, Time Management, Proper Planning, Hard work, and determination. I used to always tell my students that I'm extremely proud of my basketball career. I haven't been cut from a team since the third grade. Even I wasn't the star on a team, I was blessed to be able to play with some of the best of the best. I didn't take a summer off from training until I went through my identity crisis in high school and then after that never again unless I was hurt. Every year I came back a better player whether it was physically or mentally. I learned that when you are an athlete your season is year-round, it does not stop! A lot of kids are in the situation where they have this natural athletic ability or a naturally good at the sport and the problem with this generation is we're feeding into the natural ability and it's a growing terrible ego. The growth of the ego is why we have the athletes that you can't tell them anything. Then when they get in a situation where they get to a college and they're not the best player at the school they don't survive. It's a shock to the ego that we as coaches, fans and communities have created. Humbleness usually comes by force. Kids are coming home more broken than they were when they left because we are more focused on what they are doing for our program now. Our job is to build a respectable athlete who will grow into a respectable citizen whether they have a ball in their hand or not. The lessons that I got from basketball I still carry in my regular life because my coaches made sure to teach us life lessons in connection with the sport. They knew this wouldn't last forever but the lessons learned would.

Free Game:

- *Understand that college is a business*
- *Books and sports go hand in hand*
- *Internships are more important than the degree*
- *Contracts are yearly not for all 4 years at once (Not Guaranteed)*
- *Know what type of student you are when picking a college(big school v. Small school)*
- *Sometimes plans change*
- *Know how to balance playtime with play-time*
- *Require more of yourself than your state or your hs coach does in the classroom*
- *Know that this can be taken away and you'll be a street legend.*
- *For most kids the goal isn't to go pro.. the goal is to get a foundation laid Rather that's through a degree or networking.*
- *Never stop working even when you don't know what He's working*
- *Handle your recruiting humbly*
- *Mental health is key to physical health.*
- *Comparison is the Father of defeat. What God has for you is for you.*

8

What's Next?

They didn't tell us (Free Game Chapter)

Sports is what we do, not who we are

Sometimes chasing dreams means sacrificing things that you may be unaware of

The degree doesn't guarantee the job.

Financial stability/ credit is important to build even while in college.

Purpose is not found in how much you make.

Identity crisis for an athlete post-college career

When you play a sport for most of your life, you don't understand how much that sport becomes a part of you. The sport is your place of solace. The sport is how people remember you. If you never do anything else big in your life, your sport and what you gave to it will always live on through the people there to experience it. But the truth is we can't stay in that place. Most people who grow up playing sports don't go on to play pro. So at some point, they have to accept that that phase of their life will eventually end. The sooner they can accept that, the better and smoother that transition has the possibility of being. Not saying the transition will be perfect, but it won't be as bad as other people who go through it. Kids often become too consumed with a sport at such an early age they can forget that the sport is extra to their life.. not their life. This is how kids often excel well on the court or field but struggle in the classroom. This is also why you have certain students who can only keep their grades up while they're in season or right before the Season to make sure they can play their sport.

But aside from those little connections to the over-importance of a sport in most athletes' lives, what no one tells you about is the identity crisis you go through once that phase of your life is over. Rather your career ends in High school or college; I think most athletes can agree it is not an easy transition into this being a "regular person" thing. For so much time of our life, this sport has taken up space and given purpose. The discipline of waking up for early practices or taking care of your body even in the off-season are things that can still be used even when the sport is done. Most athletes spend those first couple of months after being done trying to figure out what to do with all this free time. For years we have committed ourselves to a sport, and now we have all of this free time, so the first thing we usually do is...Nothing. Yep, you read that right. Those first couple of days to a week are filled with video games, TV, junk food, time with friends and family, and sleep. We intentionally don't work out because we've been working out all this time, so what's a few days or weeks? (Side note: Don't do it!! Don't stop working out). This is our first step back into normalcy, but that's literally only the beginning of the identity battle.

So what most people don't realize is that being a student-athlete, especially for a long time, keeps you coddled. Most student-athletes don't have the time to work a job because school and their sport are full-time and let's be honest, most coaches, especially on the Collegiate level feel as though they are paying for you to go to school that is your job. This keeps us from getting a lot of work experience or life experience for that matter. Unless you have a family educated on financial literacy, this is often where we make some of our worst financial decisions because you are just there enjoying the experience and consumed with the grind.

Most kids from the inner city, when on scholarship, school is paid for, but other expenses are not. So that leads them to take out loans without any concern or thought of how they will pay them back. This is also a time where most students should be developing their credit to be in a decent position once they are done with school. But again, this is not what is taught to us when we go through the recruitment process or during our development as a student. We put more value on getting good grades so that we can play or so that we can graduate. I think we should be putting more value in teaching the survival things needed once both of these phases of our lives is over. So overall, these are the common battles of those whose careers come to an end. Now, this thing that has been such a part of me is no longer there. Ok, how can I replace it? I went to school and got this degree. How do I use it? Then what if I went to school for something that I really wasn't interested in, but it made it easier on me with sports? A lot of athletes find themselves in a depression just off small thoughts like these. Your friends have either started careers or figured out how to make some money, so they are now buying houses and seem to be light years ahead of you in life right now.

Anxiety kicks in; you start feeling like you are behind in life because you have spent all these years playing a sport, and when you get done with school, you have nothing to show for it, other than the piece of paper. At this point, I realized that the very thing that was preached to us was a lie. " Go to college and get a good job" that's not the formula for success. Because in my eyes, I did everything right and still didn't know what was truly next for me after school. This is the point where I learned a degree is not what gets you the job. The reality is jobs are not impressed about you having a degree on your resume but no work experience connected to it. The other reality is everybody is not built to work for someone else. So don't box yourself and think you are only good enough to be an employee. If you have taken the time to go to school and learn or take up a trade or even self educate yourself on something you find interesting, then take the risk and bet on yourself. Coming to the end of your career brings the confusion of not knowing what's next but it also shows where your focus has been during the time of being an student athlete.

The journey afterlife of an athlete can be a complicated yet fulfilling one. It's honestly all about your perception of what's going on around you. You have a few choices, you can stay stuck in the past or what's coming to an end and find yourself falling into a depression, or you can prepare to close out one chapter of your life while preparing for the start of the next. When I accepted my career was over, I went through a phase where I didn't even want to coach. I didn't want to coach because I no longer wanted to be identified with basketball. I had been playing ball since I was In the 4th grade, so that's what most people knew of me. I wanted others to see it was more to me than that, but I wanted to see it even for myself.

Lessons Learned

This chapter is not for everyone. This chapter was a part of my life that I learned from experience on two different sides. As a student-athlete, I saw countless students come to school on scholarships. Those kids didn't know the difference between a full and partial, so they ended up having to take out loans and cover the rest of school. This lack of education, in the beginning, would cost them thousands of dollars while still not understanding the small things during their college years that would benefit them on the back end. I also saw this side as a teacher and coach who watched kids have these college dreams but didn't understand how their work ethic on and off the court in high school was connected to even getting that college opportunity. All I did in this section is give small pieces of game that any child and any student-athlete who is trying to college should know. The things I wish someone would have told me.

Remember the lessons that sports taught you and carry that over into your real life:

-Discipline

-Order

-Time management

-Awareness of your circle

-Hard work

-Commitment

These things will still need to be groomed as you get older.

Make sure you have a plan no matter what.

- Preparation for change eases the sting.
- Start learning what some of your other passions are and how you can now start pursuing them.
- Never stop working out; the Body ages quickly.

Degree vs. work experience

Know that experience holds more weight than what you learned in the books. The degree only shows that you can sit in a classroom and listen and comprehend. It doesn't show if you can do the job or not. Most likely, the people you intern with are the people who will give you your first shot of experience.

- Try to secure an internship every year after your freshman year
- Volunteer at events that are related to your desired field. This way, you can start networking early.
- When you pick a major in school, please don't pick a major you want because you think it will make a lot of money. You are not making that money while in college, so that will not motivate you when times are hard, and you want to come home. This is where the first sight of some of your potential passions should begin to reveal themselves.

Dedication

The book is dedicated to my babies...

Nasir, Tylar, Navy, Kace, Kaiden

we are healing so that you don't have to.

to my Angels

MaryBell Smith, Lavada Smith, Tyne Smith, Trisha Murray, Debo Ciesi-olka, Butch Redmond and Geraldine Tolbert

I carry each of you with me.

and to my Parents & Village

Timika Smith, Deborah Smith, Anthony Tolbert, Robert Shaw, Will `Alexander

Thank You.